FINDING HOME

Jessica Sims

Absolute Author
Publishing House

FINDING HOME
Copyright © 2019 by Jessica Sims
All Rights Reserved

Author: Jessica Sims
Publisher: Absolute Author Publishing House
Supervising Publisher: Dr. Carol Michaels
Senior Project Editor: Dr. Melissa Caudle
Interior Designer: Dr. Melissa Caudle
Cover Designer: Rebecca Covers

Library of Congress Cataloging-Publication-Data

Sims, Jessica
   Finding Home/Jessica Sims
      p. cm.

ISBN: **978-1-951028-07-7**

1.   Biographical   2. Historical Biography

Printed in the United States of America
0 1 2 3 4 5 6 7 8 9

DEDICATION

Dear Mary,

I wrote this story for you. You always said to me, "I want you to find my daddy's people," and by the grace of God, I found home.

ACKNOWLEDGMENTS

I want to thank God and the people who made my publishing dream a reality. To God, I shout hallelujah giving You the highest praise. Thank You for being the head of my life. You brought me from a mighty long way.

To my mother, Sarah Sims, my niece, Genesis Sims, and my sister, Greta Sims, who always had more faith in me than I had in myself at times, thank each of you for your confidence and inspiration. I used to wonder if you all thought I was Wonder Woman or something because whatever I came up with you guys would say that I could. I realize it's because you love me unconditionally and want only the best for me.

To my children, Amber Sims, Ambriell Trimble, and Nigel Sims, the ones who are responsible for the gray hairs popping up all over my head, if I had to go through it all over again raising you all as a single mother, I would gladly do so. I am incredibly proud of you three and thank each of you for the encouragement.

To my two best friends in the whole world who believe that if Grandma says it, then it has to be true -- my grandchildren Amere Wade (Mere Mere) and Jessica Sims (Toot Toot). You both are my inspiration and my motivation to strive for greatness just the way your mothers and uncle did when they were your age. The only difference is that when they got on my last nerve for the day, I had to just deal with it. But, you two I can get on the phone and call your parents to come and get you. If they don't get here fast enough, I will put you in the car and take you myself. Thanks for loving Grandma.

To my stylist, Cassandra Alexander, special thanks for your unconditional support.

To the rest of my family, who believed in me, I could never thank you enough.

And, last but not least, to my editor, Dr. Melissa Caudle. There are no words to explain how grateful and thankful I am for you.

"Find Your Purpose in the true adventure of faith." **Jessica Sims**

TABLE OF CONTENTS

1. The Deed

A leaf descended from the top branch and floated softly to the ground, which marked the beginning of fall. Tomorrow and the day after, as the weather brought a chill to the air, the trees would soon be bare, and the rain would come too.

John Oscar Chambless, sixteen, barefoot and dressed in ragged blue jeans and a dingy oversized white shirt with holes sat beneath a giant tree and watched each leaf skate on air until they landed. Each time a leaf fell, he lifted his toes. This tree brought comfort and provided a safety net for him. One thing he was bent on was not ever being caught by those dirty White boys who had run him down like a pack of scent hounds leading hunters on a chase to kill their game. If he had to die, John was not going out without a fight. John's personality was like that of a honey badger, ferocious for his small size. Even if it meant he had to do the unthinkable, the unimaginable, the unheard of.

FINDING HOME

One night, late in September, John smelled the scent of those White men who violently held him to the ground and beat him. Young John, barefoot, hadn't done anything different that evening as he walked along the long dirt road headed for home. When an old-rusted red pickup truck pulled up beside him, the brakes squealed as the truck came to a stop.

The White driver's yellow stained teeth told his story of neglect as he rolled down the window. "What you doing out here, boy?" His words slurred drunkenly. "You know it ain't safe for your kind to be caught walking by yourself at night."

John's stomach knotted and felt like a brick as if it hit the ground. He kept his head down, his mahogany brown eyes to the ground, as he continued to walk because he knew, either way, he was in trouble.

The second passenger who sat in the middle of the seat bench leaned closer to the window. "Hey boy, you hear us talking to you?" He chugged a bottle of whiskey and belched.

John tilted his nose in the air as the smell of the whiskey pouring from the truck polluted the air. *Just what I need, drunken White boys.* He continued his path, hoping they would leave him alone. As he lengthened his stride, an empty whiskey bottle hit John in the face. He knew that the stuff running down was not sweat because it was warm and felt different. John ignored the assault and increased his pace.

Two of the White boys leaped out of the truck and bolted toward John.

John glanced over his shoulder as fear swept through his veins. "Look, I don't want no trouble." His heart thrummed against his boney ribcage.

The driver flashed a sinister grin. "You just found some a whole lot of it."

John dashed toward the woods as the two who were once passengers chased after him.

The driver slammed the gas pedal as road rocks sprayed the area, kicking up dust. "I'm comin' for you boy." He spat out the truck window. When he got beside John, he lobbed another whiskey bottle at him, but missed, as John sprinted into the woods.

The other two pursued him as if John was their last meal's entertainment.

The driver hopped out of the truck and dashed toward the three to catch them. "Get back here, boy! You can't escape. You never can."

John jumped over logs, twigs, and rocks making his escape, but his energy drained and the two boys caught John. The larger boy chunked his whiskey bottle at John's head, slowing him down a bit.

The larger boy gained the distance needed to trap John and tightly wrapped his arm around his victim's neck, choking him as he glared at his friend who drove the truck. "Go back to the truck. Keep a watch out! We don't need no trouble."

As the larger boy grappled John, the other slammed his fist into his stomach.

John broke free and wildly punched at his assailants connecting his fist into his captive's cheekbone. To John,

3

everything seemed to be in slow motion as the attack continued. For every punch the boys landed, John punched back with the power of a death-stalker scorpion, the worst of any scorpion on earth having the impact as if being trampled by an elephant.

The boys finally controlled John holding him to the ground. His breath fast and beads of sweat covered his brow and upper lip.

Smack! The boys delivered punch after punch which landed on John's face. Thump! Another into his stomach. Splat! Several into his torso and legs. Thud! He fought with all his strength and for a quick second, broke one arm free from the boy's grasp. Out of the corner of his eye, the whiskey bottle barely glimmered in the moonlight. *There is a God.* He snatched the glass bottle, struck it on a rock breaking the pour spout, and then slashed one of the boy's throat. He raised the bottle toward the remaining assailant and kicked him off.

The boy landed two feet away on a rock. He quickly rose and bolted toward the road.

Outraged, John's hand fisted until his knuckles turned white. *I can't let them get gone. They'll kill me for sure.* He grabbed the only weapon near to him, the broken whiskey bottle, and chased after them with the speed of a black panther.

The boy tripped over a rock, stumbling to the ground. Crack! The snap of his leg bone seemed to echo throughout the woods as he landed in a prone position. "Damn, I broke my leg. I'm going to kill you, boy!" He attempted to rise but couldn't.

John, seething, stood glaring over him. "You better think twice before ever laying a hand on me." John lifted the broken whiskey bottle.

The White boy's eyes darted quickly in fear. "You can't kill me. You don't have the nerve."

Smack! John struck the bottle across the boy's temple; blood splattered onto his face and torn shirt. The crimson fluid oozed from the head wound. "Now, who don't have no nerve?"

The boy gasped and took his last breath giving John the last word.

John gawked out of breath for about a minute at the dead bodies; then, he escaped the scene of the crime. John didn't know where his legs and feet were taking him; he blindly kept running as tears streamed down his face clearing a path through the dirt and smudge. It felt like forever when he reached a river. He examined the area for the best way across. He sludged through a portion, over a log, a rock and managed to reach the other side. With not a second to lose, he increased his pace.

It wasn't long in the distance the roar of a freight train drew closer to John's position. The train's whistle blew at a crossing, and it was as if his mother, Fannie, called to him. "Get on that train baby, go start a life, and never come back."

John's childhood memories flashed before him as he sprinted closer toward the train track. *I'm a-going Momma*. It felt like he would never reach those tracks. Conflicted, he questioned his actions. *Should I turn*

5

*around? No, run, they'll kill me. I deserve to die. I just
killed two White boys. No, run, do what Mamma said.*

"Don't stop baby keep running. Get far away as you
can. Run!"

God must have been with John because when he
reached a clearing the train yard was twenty feet ahead.
A train slowly pulled away. He dodged for the train,
although it was extremely painful because his feet were
swollen and cut from running barefoot. As he got close to
the open train, two White hands reached out to grab him.
He turned around, but his father, Jonathan, seemed to
speak to him from the beyond. "It's okay Son, go on."

John grabbed the hands, which pulled him inside the
train's car. With his hands on his knees, he gazed upward
at three White boys. He thought his heart raced before;
now, it seemed as if it were on the outside of his chest.
The blood in his veins pulsated.

The first White boy grinned. "Where you going?"

"Where you come from?" The second White boy
pointed toward the woods.

"You got a name?" The third White boy lifted his
thick brows inquisitively.

John still shocked and frightened by the assault and
him killing the two White boys trembled. His stomach
growled.

"In just a ways up, there's a jungle or a camp for
hobos. You can get off there."

"I'm gonna stay put and get me some distance."

"Boy, you got trouble following you?"

"Don't matter if you do, we all got trouble behind us." The second boy grinned.

"I need to get as far away as I can." *Trouble isn't the word for what I've done.*

2. The Camp

A couple of hours later, the train stopped in Manchester, Georgia and John leaped off. Ahead, was a large tree which provided shade. He sat beneath it as a gust of wind rustled the leaves. He shivered and wrapped his arms over his chest and turned his front toward the tree in hopes it would block the chilly breeze. His stomach growled as his brow scowled. *I'm in a whole lot of deep trouble. How long will it take for those White men to catch me and find out my name? Will they kill my family? Momma, what do I do?*

Don't you worry about us, baby, you are a man, it's time for you to fend for yourself. His mother's voice in his head seemed to calm him.

John looked over his shoulder, hoping to see his mother, but instead, he visualized his father, who stood next to him.

"Son, a real man takes care of himself, and you need to; no matter what."

"Yes, Pappa. I'll never go back, but if I do, I'll show you and Momma a different man. You'll see what I'll do out on my own. I'll make you proud."

Suddenly, a jungle buzzard, a dark-skinned resident who lived at the camp, eased up to John. "Hello, I'm Irene. What's your name, boy?" Her sixty-year-old body had seen better days. She moved closer and studied him. "What have you done that's got you all shaken up and scared? You look like you killed a White man or something."

John gazed at Irene with his big, brown, bloodshot eyes and gulped.

"You can't hide the blood of a White man. By the looks of you, you've been in a nasty fight."

His eyes widened as his heart pounded.

She smirked. "I don't wanna know nothin' at all. Whatever it is, is better not told."

Relieved, John smiled. "Thank you."

"You'd best be forgettin' about it too. What do they call you in these parts?"

"John."

"Okay, John it is. Now, take off your clothes and let them dry by the fire."

"I have nothin' underneath but my drawers."

"Once you seen one pair, you be seeing them all. Take off your clothes and go sit by the fire and warm your skinny self up."

John sighed as he began to undress. *Maybe I can stop running now.*

For the first time, it seemed like that swarm of bumblebees stinging his head stopped circling. Terrified, his heart still raced, but he swore he heard his mother's soft voice. "Now, my sweet son, go do what you have to do in this life to take care of yourself. I may never see you again but know that I will always be with you in spirit. Remember to put God first, Son."

He lifted his eyes toward the heavens as he sighed.

"No matter what lies ahead, Son, always put God first, He will work it out. There will be crying times as well as trying times, but as long as you put Him first, you will be all right."

John felt a warmness from Irene, which reminded him of his mother. Her uncanny resemblance, short, dark-skinned, with long black hair like silk, softened his heart toward the jungle buzzard.

The calmness of Irene's voice made John finally realize that it had been two whole days, and he hadn't eaten anything. As if on cue, John's stomach growled, the world around him blurred for a moment.

Irene took notice right away. "You best be gettin' into bed. Go ahead. Take a nap in my tent while your clothes dry. Now undress."

John entered the tent, and one at a time he handed an article of clothing through the tent opening to his new friend.

Irene walked south toward the stream.

***

Most of the hobos who took walks or scrounged for scraps meandered back into the camp. Irene, holding John's clean and dried clothes, quickly strode toward her tent. She stood by the opening. "John, your clothes be dry. Get dressed." She tossed the clothes through the opening.

"Thank you, Ms. Irene," drifted from inside the tent.

John, dressed, exited, and studied the camp. A smile crossed his lips as he observed several hobos gambling, and his eyes lit up like the stars in the sky because one thing John Chambless knew was how gamble.

Irene snickered. "You a gamblin' man?"

"Me and my brothers are known for breaking any house game.

"You don't say?"

"People would leave the game if one of us Chambless boys showed up and heaven forbid more than one of us show up, that was all she wrote."

"Then get yourself into that game. Those fools know how to lose money they don't got."

"One problem. I don't have a single penny to my name?" He looked down at his bare feet. "I can't even put my shoes in cause I ain't got none. Don't you go worrying yourself about me. I always figure something out."

The sweet aroma of apple pies drifted his way. "That smells exactly like the ones my mother would bake on Saturday evenings." He sniffed the air and savored the smell. "Well, that is except those she made from peaches I stole from the White boy's farm."

"Sounds like she liked to bake."

"Bake doesn't do her pies justice. Every Sunday she took two apple pies and seven peach pies to church to share with the others. She always hid two others for us to eat after dinner." His stomach rumbled and growled.

"Sounds like you could use a piece. Go ahead. Find out where they be. They won't fill your tummy from over here."

John's bare feet moved as though they had a mind of their own as he walked toward the sweet aroma and stopped at the back door of a cafe. John huffed when he noticed a delivery truck filled with pies. "That's where you're coming from."

"Hey boy, what are you doing back here?" The owner, covered in flour over his apron and hat, headed his way.

John's first instinct was to run, but his energy failed him. "Nothin' sir. Just admiring the smell. They smell like my mothers.

"You look hungry. I'll make you a deal. You load this truck, and I'll give you something to eat."

As hunger pains shot through his stomach and his taste buds churned, John spent the next three hours loading the pies.

From the back door, the owner checked on his progress. When John loaded the last batch, the owner waved him to the door. "Good job." He pointed to a milk crate. "Now sit right here, and I'll send some food your way."

As the door slammed shut, John sat. He twiddled his thumbs and hummed an unfamiliar tune. Soon, a waitress carrying a tray exited and sat it down at his feet. "These are for your work."

"That's mighty kind of you miss. Looks good. I love me some chicken and dumplings, corn on the cob, sweet peas and a cold glass of sweet tea."

"Eat it before it gets cold." She entered the backdoor. It slammed behind her.

John gobbled his food without haste. He wasn't sure if it was because the food was that delicious, or he was that hungry.

The backdoor swung open. "This one is for the road." The owner handed John an apple pie. "This is what brought you here, you should leave with it."

"Thank you, sir. I won't let a bite go wasted from this mighty fine pie."

"Come back tomorrow, and I will have more work for you."

John beamed a smile. "Yes, sir. Bright and early. I won't let you down."

"You're a hard worker. I could use help like you around here."

"I don't mean to sound greedy because I'm awfully thankful for the work. You think you can pocket me some cash too for a good day's work?"

"I'll see what I can do. No promises."

Earning food and smelling the pies momentarily gave John a reprieve from the trouble he left behind in Monroe, Georgia. Carefully holding the apple pie, he limped to Irene's tent.

"Now looky here. Where did you get that pie?"

"I got a job loading them. I got fed too. You can have half, but I have plans for the other half."

"Look at you now. In one day, you earned yourself a pie, a job, and a place to stay."

"I got no place to stay."

"You can hold up here with me as long as you keep bringing me pie, but you have to find your own food. I ain't got enough for myself."

"You got yourself a tent mate. I'm a natural-born hustler and a fast talker too. That comes from the Geechee."

"Geechee? What's a Geechee?"

"My folks come from the Geechee area from West Africa. We're hard-working people. I'll earn a little cash and gamble to get more. Besides, I'm a God-fearing man because my mother was a God-fearing woman."

"I'm not so sure about that God of yours."

John's eyes diverted toward his feet. Deep down inside, he questioned if God was real, and if He is, why did he let his people suffer? Why did God allow his people to leave Africa by ship to be servants in a foreign land?

Then his mother's words comforted his anguish. "God loves all people."

Irene tapped him on the shoulder. "You look like you got a lot on your mind."

"Yep. Way too much."

"A penny for your thoughts."

"I can't help but wonder why no Africans got together, built boats, and came to see where they took their people. What would have happened if they did?

"That's some kind of heavy thinking for any troubled mind."

"Think about it. If the people who were enslaved weren't Africans at all, and they were just the same skin color, or they were foreigners in Africa stolen by the Africans sold by the Africans to other foreigners."

"You need to erase all those thoughts from your head and be thankful you got a means to eat and a tent over your head."

"How about that half of the pie I promised?"

She gladly took the pie, fumbled for a knife, and cut it in half. She found a dirty cooking pan and dumped her half into it.

John then took the other half and cut four slices. He wryly grinned as he glanced toward the hobo's gambling across the camp. His stride increased as he carefully held the pie. When he arrived at the gamblers, he waved the pie beneath their noses. "Take a whiff. Fresh today."

Each hobo sniffed the pie and licked their lips.

"I got slices of pie, fifteen cents each."

The chubby rosy cheeked gambler dug in his coat pocket. "Found it." He handed John a dime and a nickel.

John slammed the coins onto the table. "Mind if I lose my money to you?"

The other hobos laughed.

"It's your money to lose." The chubby hobo took a huge bite of his pie.

Hours passed as the gambling continued until the wee hours of the morning. John stretched, then put on a pair of shoes he won. "Thanks, I'll take care of these."

"You better, it's the last pair I got."

John strolled toward Irene's tent. She smiled at him. "I've been watching you. You're as good as you say you are."

"I don't tell a lie. I just might not say nothin' at all."

"If you keep this up, you can stay here as long as life allows."

"If I do that, you won't ever go hungry again as long as I'm breathing."

"How much did you win?"

"Besides these shoes, two whole dollars."

"Not bad for your first day. You must be pretty smart."

"I got as much education as most. Made it up to the eighth grade. I can read and write and count my money too. Really, countin' my money is the only thing I need. Nobody can cheat me if I can count money."

Irene wiped the pie crust from her lips. "That was a mighty fine pie."

"I don't take from anybody, less they take from me. Unless it's gambling, then all's fair. If they're stupid enough to play, they're stupid enough to lose. My momma always says do unto others as you have them do unto you but, I will do unto others as they do unto me. I mean it too. You can ask that overseer I put in his place."

"Boy, what are you talkin' about?"

"I once worked in the field, picking peaches. One day, this man, who had been working all day without as much as a cup of water to drink, was confronted about the number of peaches he picked. When he turned in his bags

16

to get paid, the overseer laughed at him. This all you got? Two bags? Boy, this ain't enough to do nothing with. Go on home, come back tomorrow, and try again. The old man begged them to pay him because he had a family to feed."

"They killed him, didn't they?"

"No. They didn't care about his reason or his hungry family. My temper got the best of me. I balled up my fists and stuffed them in my pockets. Sweat rolled down my face. I wanted to beat the living daylights out of those two overseers."

"Well, did you?"

"No, I felt bad about it, but I knew if I did, I wouldn't get paid and get killed too."

"So, you're not as tough as you say you are."

"Don't get me wrong. I didn't do anything right then, but later that evening, when I was walking home, I couldn't get the old man and the overseers out of my mind. The story goes like this."

***

John approached a truck full of peaches parked on the side of the back-country road. Unsure whom it belonged too, he hid in the brush and waited. The last thing he needed was to get caught by White men. You die that way, and he knew it. He had to be extra careful not to be seen.

He waited, pondering his next move. If nobody saw him and nobody heard him, and if that truck and peaches belonged to the overseer, he'd steal them.

Then a car drove by so John ducked off into the woods far enough to be out of sight. Patiently, he waited and observed; he must be sure that the truck and the peaches belonged to the overseer.

John's eyes widened as confidence swelled inside.

The car horn blared, and the driver exited. As the man walked to the back of the truck, the two overseers, drunk as Cooter Brown, came from the opposite side of the woods. A drunk woman flanked each one. The foursome walked to the back of the truck where the man waited. The man lifted the covering from the bed of the truck, and handed the boys two mason crates, then he reached back, and retrieved a mason jar out of one of the containers.

"This is the best moonshine the South has to offer. Now get on down the road and drop this stuff off if you want to get paid." He got back into his truck and drove off as the boys put the crates on the back of the truck with the peaches. Laughing and staggering, they got a bottle out of one of the crates and started drinking as they headed into the woods.

John sat in silence to make sure the men were far enough into the woods so they couldn't hear him. He took off his shoes and bolted toward the old gambling house owned by Ms. Sadie, the bootlegger down the road.

When John arrived, he looked for his brother, who was engaged in a craps game with his best friend, Jimmy. He ordered a hot mullet fish sandwich and approached the game. He bent to eye level with his brother. "You're not going to believe what I saw."

"Not now, John, I'm busy."

"You'll want to know about the moonshine."

"Moonshine!"

"Shhh."

Ms. Sadie headed their way with John's sandwich. "You want something to drink? And, I don't mean no soda."

"Not today. I got chores tomorrow. Need a clear mind that white lightning clogs."

When John finished his sandwich, he, his brother, and Jimmy left. John knew that if the three of them went together, and when or if it got out that someone had robbed the White boys, they would be at the top of the list of suspects.

John leaned into his brother's ear. "Meet me in the woods. Don't say a word."

His brother nodded, and he and Jimmy left.

John gave them a couple of minutes to get a head start. He passed Ms. Sadie on the way out. "Best sandwiches this side of the Mississippi."

She beamed a toothless smile.

"Ms. Sadie. I need a favor. You got any of them mason jars I could borrow?"

"What they for?"

"I need to steal me some moonshine. Someone is stomping on your ground."

"How many do you need?"

"A crate."

"Stay here." Ms. Sadie left and returned within seven minutes. "I filled them with water. It'll look like moonshine. That way they won't notice what's missing."

"I knew I liked you for a reason."

"Just be careful. Stealing from the White boys will get you into a heap of trouble if not a tarring or hanging."

John nodded in confirmation and left.

When John arrived at the truck, he belted a huge sigh of relief because it was still there filled with the moonshine. He strode down the road toward the location of the truck on the side of the road and waited in the woods. where he had told his brother and Jimmy to meet him. He paced because it was taking Jimmy and his brother too long, so he started running back and forth across the street switching the jars of moonshine with the jars of water. Before long, John exchanged an entire crate. "This is for you, old man.

He snatched a crate of peaches bolted back into the woods. Out of breath, footsteps rustled near. He looked over his shoulder and to his relief it was his brother and Jimmy. "About time you showed. I was getting worried."

"We made sure no one followed. So, we're stealing peaches too."

"Why not? Looks like a whole lot of Momma's peach pie."

"I'm in."

"Then don't stand there, we got moonshine and peaches to tote."

"Momma will tear the skin off your back if you come home with moonshine and these peaches. You know how she feels about liquor and stealing."

"We'll take them to Ms. Sadie's. We'll strike a deal with her."

"What kind of deal do you offer a bootlegger?"

"Moonshine. We'll pay her to sell the stuff. Everyone profits. I can count the money now."

"I can count the peach pies."

The boys all laughed.

"Now the real plan for the peaches. We dole them out. We give the old man his fair share and the rest of the crew theirs. We'll sneak some home to Momma."

A few days later, the old man carrying a peach pie went to visit John who sat on the porch chewing on a broom straw, like he always did. He handed John the peach pie. "My wife insisted on making you the first pie for your trouble. Thanks for the help."

"That's the least I could do. I wasn't about to let that overseer take your hard-earned money. None of us make enough as it is."

"Thanks, again, John. Your momma raised you right."

"That's because she's a God-fearing woman."

About an hour later, John's next-door neighbor came and brought him a peach pie; then another and another, and before long, he had nine peach pies. He went inside to take the peach pies, and when he got in the kitchen, he smelled a sweet aroma. John's mother pulled another peach pie from the oven. "Smells like heaven, Momma."

"No, Son. Heaven is going to smell sweeter. You can count on it."

John sat the other pies on the table, and his brother and Jimmy entered the kitchen. When they gazed at all ten pies, they laughed.

Jimmy laughed so hard he had tears streaming down his face. "Let's call this man pie."

***

Irene smiled as she took the last bite of her peach pie. "That was some long peach pie story."

"Yea, but I got em' back. Nobody steps on me. You do right by me; I'll do right by you."

"Or, I'll steal your moonshine and peaches."

"You know it."

"It's time to close your eyes. You got work in the morning."

"It has been a rather long twenty-four hours. Which side of the tent you want?"

"My side. The one with the dirty pillow."

John nodded. "As soon as I have spare money, I'll buy you a new one. I'll get me one too."

"Don't promise nothin' you can't deliver."

"I would never. I'm an honest God-fearing man. My momma taught me that way."

3. The Dream

Manchester Georgia proved to be a great landing place for John. He earned enough wages working for the owner at the café washing dishes and loading the delivery truck. Every day, he returned to the tent with something to eat for him and Irene and about seventy-five cents in his pocket, which he hid in a dirty sock inside Irene's tent. His goal was to save enough money to head north, gain employment, and send for his family. He desired nothing more than to get them out of the south, where they treated Black folk like trash.

Night drew close as the hobos gathered around the fire to stay warm. The chubby gambler nudged John. "Your plans are good. People up north treat Blacks different."

"Why you suppose that is?"

"Ever heard of emancipation? They fought to free the slaves."

"I don't need no history lesson. I learned that in the sixth grade."

"What's your real plan?"

"I want a taste of that freedom for me and my family. I can't go north empty-handed, and I don't want to hop on a train the same way I got here."

"That's some mighty big dreams."

"That's not all. I'm gonna buy me a clean suit, wear me some suspenders, put on a silk tie and dress shoes. I'm gonna get a hat to match."

"Are you sure those aren't pipe dreams. You're a poor Black man washing dishes. A crisp new suit don't seem to fit in that picture."

Irene laughed. "Leave him alone. He knows what he wants. A man has to have a dream."

"That's right. I cut me out some pictures of the fancy suits I want. That way, when I have enough money, I can show the store exactly what I want."

"You do that, and you'll look like a fancy White boy."

"Mine will be better and more flashy. They'll know I'm somebody when they see me coming. I'll even stand out against those rich White boys who ran away that I see riding the trains."

"Keep dreaming."

"Man, where do you think I'm getting most of my money. They get off the train to look around and the next thing they know, they're gambling with me, and I take them to the house."

John had it all figured out; he was going to have a pocket full of money, a suitcase full of fancy clothes, then head to the bus station for a one-way ticket straight to New York City or Detroit, Michigan. It didn't matter to him if he left the south behind him.

"You wait and see. One day I'll come back here to this camp driving up in my fancy new car. I'll even take Irene to lunch in it. I'll show you and my family what a fine man I have become living in the big city."

Irene smiled. "I look forward to it. Come on, John, you have another big day, and it's late. I want to go to sleep."

The chubby gambler's brow creased. "Just because you want to go to bed, doesn't mean we can't win our money back from John."

"Nope! He wakes me up when he comes in late, and it's my tent."

John stood. "Goodnight, everyone."

Irene and John made their way into the tent and plopped down onto their ragged bedding. Irene propped her head on her tattered pillow. "When you're that big man from the city, bring me a goose down feather pillow. The ones the rich people sleep with."

"You can count on it."

For a moment, the crickets overpowered the silence. John stared up toward the top of the tent lit by the moonlight. The glow of the fire created a warm ambiance. John grabbed a bottle of whiskey, took a swig, and handed it to Irene. "Want to brush your teeth."

She grabbed the bottle and gulped a mouthful and handed it back to him.

"Why did you let me stay with you?"

"You remind me of my son."

"What happened to him? Did he die?"

"No, my boy ain't dead, but he always had anger in his heart toward Whites ever since he was a boy. I suppose he had a good reason. Yes."

"What was that?"

"When he was five or six, he saw a White man slap his grandfather across the face. He loved his grandpa more than life itself. It crushed him and built his hatred."

"That's a tough thing for any kid to see."

"It got worse."

"How could it? Getting slapped is pretty harsh enough."

"Tyrone, that's my son, was walking to the store one day with Brenda, that's his sister, and some White boys came up riding in a truck. One of the White boys picked his sister up and threw her on the back of it and drove off."

"I'm beginning to see things must have gotten really heated."

"It was about two weeks later when they found my baby's body floating in the Chattahoochee River." Irene's voice quivered as tears rolled down her face.

"A White boy would have to die if they did that to my sister."

"They just said my baby drowned, but I saw those marks around her neck and my Tyrone, he swore to me that he would take care of everything. He told me not to worry because he was going to do it for Brenda. He wouldn't listen to me. I begged him to let it alone. He didn't get it. I already have one dead child; I didn't want another. You know what he said?"

John shook his head and took another swig.

"Momma, you can't wait on God for everything." Irene licked her lips and wiped her tears.

"I begged him to let things be. Then one night, about five or six years later, Tyrone came home with that same look in his eyes that you had the first time I saw you. That blank stare; that look, I will never forget long as I live. He told me that we had to go, and we couldn't take anything but the clothes we had on our backs."

"Did you go?"

"I knew by the look in Tyrone's eyes that it was something serious, so I got up and put my shoes on. He grabbed my hand and, on the way, out, he knocked over every kerosene lamp in the house, setting it on fire. He dragged me out of the house and told me don't look back."

"I'm so sorry. You don't deserve any of this."

"Deserving ain't got nothing to do with it."

"Where do ya'll go?"

"Next thing I know, we was in the woods by a train station. That's when I asked him why we had to leave on the run."

"Don't tell me. He killed somebody."

"Not just anybody. He saw the man that pulled his sister up on the truck, shot him dead and threw his body in the river. The same river they found my sweet Brenda in."

"That explains why ya'll left so quick. So, where did you two go?"

"Tyrone insisted I get on one train going in one direction, and he got on one going another way. When things calmed down, we were supposed to meet up. He said he'd find me if it were God's will."

"Have you ever seen your son, since the train?"

"He was only sixteen. He was just a baby. Part of me knew he was right, and the other part said I needed to go with him. He wouldn't listen. He said he was a man and that God would take care of him better than I ever could."

"That explains how you got here."

"It was the first stop I came to and believed he would find me."

"So, how long has it been?"

"I stopped counting ten years ago, but I had reason to stay put."

"Hope. The hope your son would find you, right?"

"That, and about eight years ago, a hobo came through from New York and gave me a message. He said, he knew Tyrone, and he told him that if he ever came across a thin, dark-skinned woman nearly forty years old and she said she had a son by the name of Tyrone to tell her that he is okay. He also added that Tyrone was living in New York working, and he was going to come for me."

"That's a glimmer of hope. At least you heard from him."

"Better than a glimmer. I wrote him a letter because the hobo said he was heading back up that way and he'd give it to Tyrone. That's why I'll never leave here, no matter what."

"Why didn't you just follow the hobo back to New York?"

"There would be no guarantee he'd be there. One of needed to stay put to find each other."

John gulped and took a deep breath. "There's always hope."

"I will look into my son's eyes again. Whether it is down here or on the other side, I will see my boy again."

"I believe you. I pray my mamma feels the same way about me. I want to see my momma's eyes again and taste her apple pie, but if she finds out why I'm on the run, she'll never look at me the same."

"John, listen to me. The last thing I told my son was baby you gotta ask God to forgive you for what you have done, and you gotta forgive that man or else you gonna be in deep trouble with the Lord."

"I don't think I ever will."

"Before I parted ways with my baby, I made sure he had gotten things right with God. You need to do the same thing before you head off in those fancy clothes and shoes. If you ain't right with the Lord, you ain't right."

John twiddled his thumbs as he contemplated. "Ms. Irene, what did you do back home?"

"I was a schoolteacher. Education is one of the most important things you need in life to get ahead."

"You're preaching to the choir. My momma and pappa valued education because growing up; they weren't allowed to go to school."

"That explains your ability to count."

"I think gambling has more to do with that, than my eighth-grade education." John yawned and stretched.

"Goodnight, John. It's time to close your eyes."

"Thank you, Ms. Irene, for taking me in. You're a God-fearing woman, just like my momma. If she met you, she'd love you."

"I'm sure I'd love her too. What are your plans for Christmas?"

"I guess like everyone else. Try to stay warm and fed."

"Merry Christmas."

"Yea, merry Christmas." *Some Christmas this is.*

John closed his eyes. He tossed one way, then to the other. *Maybe I should try to go see my momma. I know staying here can't be the plan God has for me.* He tossed again and rubbed his eyes. *I could write her a letter with no return address. No, I can't do that. They could be checking her mail to see where I am. I've never been so homesick in my life.*

4. The City Slicker

J ohn, outback loading dozens of pies onto the delivery truck took a deep breath. "Another day, another dollar."

John heard the morning train as it approached blowing its whistle. The whistle would bring a smile to John's face for two reasons; one because it was time for his break, and two because it reminded him of his family that he had left behind. He would imagine one day seeing them step off that train. The train's brakes squealed as it came to a complete stop. Across the street, a bus pulled up to the station. "Like clockwork."

He leaned against the truck for his first fifteen-minutes of the day and watched the hustle and bustle of the passengers exiting their mode of transportation. Thoughts of his family are what kept him going. He was in constant fear of the White boy's family finding him, but when he heard the train's whistle, he forgot all about that.

After fifteen people exited the bus, a well-dressed Black man wearing a Fedora hat stepped down landing his brand-new designer shoes onto the gravel. He immediately wiped the bottom of both shoes.

John's forehead creased. *He's not from around these parts. Too dressed to be from here.*

One of the busboys from the kitchen carrying a large bag of trash exited the kitchen. John lifted his brow. "Look what came to town."

The busboy glanced over toward the impeccably well-dressed man. "Mighty spiffin' rags."

"I'll say. Looks like we got us a city slicker over there."

"City slicker or not, he's headin' your way. You in trouble with the law?" The busboy dropped the trash, shooed a dozen flies, and entered the backdoor.

The city slicker strode over to John, tipped his hat, and smiled. "How are you all?"

John laughed. "We're just fine. What brings you around these parts?"

"I just came to visit."

"With family?"

"Yes, my folks."

John rubbed his chin. "I know most folks around here. Who's your folks?"

The man paused for a minute, gazed at John. "Do they serve Black folk in this place?"

"They do, so long as you don't mind eating in the kitchen, Mr. fancy."

"Kitchen sounds fine. That's where the best grub is anyways."

"That and a warm piece of pie. This way."

John and the man entered through the back door.

"Everyone, we got company for lunch."

The workers briefly glanced at the city slicker and went back to work. "Don't mind them. They have a lot to do to get ready for the lunch rush. What ya want to eat?"

"That fried chicken and collard greens smells awfully tasty."

"How about a piece of our famous cornbread?"

"Sounds good."

John pointed to the corner at a small table with two chairs. "You go sit there. I'll put you a plate together."

The city slicker moseyed to the table and sat. His back was straight and rigid as he folded his hands and placed them on the table.

John prepared the meal and brought the city slicker his lunch. As the man ate, John observed him because there was something about the man that he just couldn't put his finger on. *Is he the man from Monroe County? Who is he and what is he doing here dressed like that?*

One thing John was sure about was the fact that he was not going to take his eyes off this strange man, and this man indeed was not from around there.

The man took his last bite leaving his plate almost spotless. "Boy, I ain't had cooking like this since my momma last cooked for me."

"What's your momma's name?" The man stared at him but didn't say anything.

"How far is the nearest train station?"

"Now why would a man dressed fine like yourself come to town on a bus looking for a train station?"

"You see I had a little free time, and I felt like doing something I always wanted to do, and that was ride trains for a while."

"Well, you sure ain't dressed like you fixing to hop no train. Dressed like that with a pocket full of money, and you won't make it to the first stop before you get robbed blind. What you really up to? I can tell when a man is lying by the twitch in his eyes. You can't pull nothin' over on me. I'm a gambling man myself."

"Look, my name is Tyrone, and I am looking for a woman."

"Those are in the red-light district if that's your thing."

"No, not that. I'm looking for a dark-skinned woman named Irene; she could be my mother."

"I know Irene, but she don't dress like you."

"How do you know her?"

"She took me in after I hopped a train landing here a couple months back. She's like a momma to me. She gave me hope when I felt I didn't have none."

"Do you know where I can find this Irene?"

"Sure do. I'll see her tonight. It's my birthday, and we're celebrating. You want to tag along? Before you answer, it's not exactly your type of place dressed like that."

"Matters not. I want to meet this Irene. If she's my mother, you'll be a hero.

"If your name is really Tyrone, I think she is your momma. She told me about you and how... Let's say, you left town promising to come back."

"Your folks going to be there?"

John shook his head. "Not this time, but one day soon. Don't you worry about all that. You wanna see your momma or not?"

"I do, how is she? Where can I find her?"

"Hold on to your britches city slicker. There's something you ought to know about your momma. She's had it rough and lives in a hobo camp."

Tyrone's eyes flushed. He reached in his pocket and pulled out Irene's letter she gave to the hobo who headed north. "I want to read this to you. Dear son, if this letter reaches you, the first thing I want you to know is I am alive and well. The next is I miss you more than life itself. I was so relieved to hear that you were alive and that you made it safely to the north. This spot where your friend found me is where I will be waiting for you no matter how long it takes. It gets so cold out here in winter one time I thought I saw fire freeze, then one summer morning I woke up. It was so hot; I thought we had all died and gone to Hell. It's okay, though because one day, my God will put us back together and until He does, I will be right here waiting. Either on you or the good Lord, my child, whichever one of you gets here first. So, if you come to this spot and I'm not here, I've gone home with your sister, and we will be there at the crossroads waiting for you." Tyrone glanced at John as he wiped a tear off his cheek. "Does this sound like the Irene you know?"

John, in tears, not because of the message, but because he knew deep down that the only place, he would see his mother and father, brothers and sisters or any of his family again would be at the crossroads. "The Irene I know is your momma."

5. The Quilt

Tyrone waited outback of the restaurant for John to get off work. Time seemed to stand still. He glanced at his watch every five minutes as if that would speed things up. Finally, John exited. "You ready to go see your momma?"

"Almost. I'd like to buy her a Christmas present. Where's the best place for that kind of thing?"

"I'd say around the corner. Plenty of little shops. I bet you'd find something there."

"Will you help me? I want something real nice and special that means a lot to her. She's my momma."

"She told me she used to sew quilts for you and your sister. She said they kept everybody warm."

"That's perfect. It's cold out here, and I'm sure she could use it; that is what I will get her."

"Why don't you go and get her some fabric and let her make her own?"

"Yes, I'll buy her a quilt and some material to make another one."

"She wants a new goose down pillow and a new pillowcase too."

Tyrone's brow furrowed. "Okay, a pillow and a pillowcase too."

The walk to main street toward the shop went quick. Tyrone felt his heart throb knowing he'd soon see his mother again. "You're right about the shops. Look, the general store. It'll have quilts and pillows."

They bolted across the street and into the store. The salesclerk approached. "Welcome to McRory's Five and Dime. Can I help you find anything?"

Tyrone smiled. "I'd like to buy a quilt."

"They're in the back on the left."

Tyrone tipped his hat. "Thank you, ma'am."

The two men strode toward the quilt section.

John picked up a blue patch quilt and showed it to Tyrone. "How about this?"

"Not lady enough for my momma." Tyrone picked up a quilt with pink roses and lace. "This one is perfect."

"I'm sure she'll love it." John handed him a pillow and one pink pillowcase. "I think these will match."

"Now let's find her some fabric."

They strolled the aisles until they spotted the fabric section. After scanning the section, they picked out several pieces of pink and green fabric, some with yellow flowers, some with pink flowers, and some lace.

John took a deep breath. "All this shoppin' gots me mighty thirsty." He headed straight for the liquor section and retrieved a gallon of whiskey. "It is my birthday."

"Then I'm buying, but it is for the three of us."

"That was my plan."

"Time to check out and head out."

"I'm right behind you.

***

The camp was two miles outside of town alongside the river that gave John and Tyrone a chance to chit-chat.

Tyrone's stomach churned with nervousness. "So how is my momma, man? Is she ok? I mean, I ain't seen her in years, but I still remember the last thing she said to me like it was yesterday."

"Slow down. Give a man a chance to answer. She's alive and never stopped wanting to find you. She forgives you if that means anything to you."

"More than words can say. Her last words to me were that I had to ask God to forgive me. Did she tell you?"

John didn't dare respond knowing he had skeletons in his own closet he didn't want to be revealed. *Would things have been different for me if my momma was there to tell me to ask God for forgiveness?*

The two walked in silence as John recalled a prayer his momma used to pray.

Oh! Lord, if nothing else, teach my children to trust in you with all their heart and lean not on their own understanding. Lord let them submit to you in all their ways.

John shivered, as his momma's words rang loud and clear in his mind. *I know you will make their paths straight.*

"Tyrone, hold up a minute. I got to take a leak."

"I'll wait right here."

John walked just far enough to get out of Tyrone's sight, and then dropped to his knees, and for the first time since he had learned his bedtime prayers, he desired to speak to God. "Lord, I know I shouldn't be asking you for no favors but take care of my momma and the rest of my family. I killed two White boys. Not that they didn't deserve it, but their dead bodies are by my hands. Please forgive me for killing those men and forgive me for what I did to my family by leaving. I need it in order to carry on with my life."

John got up off his knees and drew in a long, deep breath. "I feel better now." *The heavy load is lifted. Thank you, God.*

John strode back out to the road, almost dragging his feet.

Tyrone adjusted his suspenders. "Everything all right? You look a little frazzled."

"I'm good. I feel better right now than I have my whole life."

"That must have been one Hell of a piss."

More like a prayer. "Ready to meet your momma?"

The two continued their path toward the camp.

Tyrone cleared his throat. "Why is a boy as young as you not at home helping work his daddy's farm or something?"

40

"Why you ask so many questions. Besides, you ain't even told me why you got separated from your momma. How come you ain't at home working on the family farm?"

"I guess I better tell you the whole story, so my momma won't have to relive it. Sit down."

They sat on a big rock, just off the road. Tyrone removed his hat and placed it on his lap. "When I was young, I had a sister named Brenda; she was the most beautiful little girl you ever wanted to see. She had smooth, black skin just like my momma, and she used to put her hair in three long pigtails. She was always reading a book. She said she was gonna be a doctor so that she could take care of momma and buy a house bigger than any house on any plantation just for us. One day some White men did some awful things to her. They raped and killed my sister."

"I'm sorry. That must've been hard for you and your mamma.

"I watched momma walk dead for years after that. It took the life right outta her. She didn't want to live no more."

"The hope of seeing you again is what's keeping her live now."

"Let me get this off my chest." He drew in a deep breath. I spent every night vowing to find the man that killed my sister so he could make him pay.

"I think I would too."

"Sometimes I'd go fishing and ask God why He didn't take me instead. She had more to live for than me, and when she became a doctor, she could take care of momma. I swore to her that I'd find those men and kill them. So, that's what I did."

"I can't blame you for that, but you don't look like a murderer the way you're dressed."

"By the way, my name is Dr. Tyrone Jones."

John dropped his jaw in disbelief. "Hey man, if you a doctor, how come you come to town on a bus and how come you just now coming to get your momma?"

"Not that it's any of your business, but I struggled when I first got to New York. An old couple took me in and put me through school. I got a job in a free clinic. That's where I met the hobo who eventually gave me the letter from my momma."

"Everything in God's timing. That's what I've been told."

"It took me years to get that White man for killing my sister. I saw his face many times, but the timing wasn't right. You know how come I ain't back home working on my daddy's farm?"

"No, why?"

"Cause my daddy ain't got no farm."

They both started laughing.

John stood. "Ready?"

"I'm right behind you. It's really getting cold out here."

"There should be a fire at the camp to warm us up."

"Let's get us a little toddy for our body." He unscrewed the cap to the whiskey then took a gulp and handed it to John.

"We're almost there. You can see the smoke from the fire up ahead. You nervous?"

Tyrone Took another swig.

"That tells me you are."

***

Irene sat outside by the fire, waiting for John to come with whatever he had brought for her to eat that evening. Darkness had fallen. Irene sat staring at the fire as the two men approached.

"You late today, boy."

Tyrone smiled and bit his lower lip. "Yeah, I had to stop and get something for you."

Irene hadn't heard that voice in years; she diverted eyes toward Tyrone. She rubbed them in disbelief. "My child." Her voice quivered. "The good Lord brought you back to me."

"Yes, momma, He did."

"Let me look at you." She positioned herself to stand as Tyrone handed off the presents to John and assisted her to her feet. Tears rolled down her face as she wrapped her arms in a death grip around his waist. "You're a man." She pulled back and examined his clothes. "And, what a fine man you've become."

"It's good to see you momma."

"It was in God's plan, after all."

"God's timing, momma."

John cleared his throat. "I'm going to shoot some craps and give you two time alone."

Neither acknowledged as John strolled away toward the tent, put the presents in them, and proceeded quickly to the gambling pit.

"Tyrone, how did you find me?"

"I kept your letter momma. Then when the time was right, I got me a bus ticket and came on down here to get you."

"You kept your promise."

"Always momma. I love you."

"How did you wind up with John?"

"Now that's the real miracle. I must have been lucky because he was the first person I met when I got off the bus, and he led me right to you."

"Praise Jesus!"

"I brought you some gifts." Tyrone looked around for John. "John, where did you put my momma's gifts?"

"I'll get em' after this next roll." He rolled the dice crapping out with a seven. "Win some; lose some. Later boys." John strode back to the tent and retrieved the presents leaving the pillow on her bedding. *I wish I could see my momma again.* When he reached Tyrone and Irene, he handed her the gifts.

"Son, you didn't have to do that."

"I know Momma; I wanted to. Open the bags."

"Let's go by the tent."

"Lead the way."

The three made their way to the front of the tent where Irene opened her presents. When she pulled out the quilt, she rubbed her face in it and then wrapped it around her. "I love it. Thanks, Son."

"There's more, Momma."

"I see. What can it be?" She pulled out the material scraps. Puzzlement overcame her.

John touched her shoulder. "That's so you can make your own the way you used to."

"Perfect. I'll make it for you, Tyrone, so you can always have it by your side when you go back home."

"Momma, I'm not leaving you here. In fact, we're not sleeping here tonight either. We're gonna find us a fancy hotel and get you a proper meal, a proper bath, and a proper bed. Nothing is too good for my momma."

Irene laughed. "Nowhere around here gonna let no colored folk stay in no hotel, Son."

"We're just going to have to find out. I done got used to a bed and a roof over my head," Tyrone explained.

She stared at him and gave him the once over. "What do you do that allows you to wear such fine clothes?"

"You'll be proud. I did it for Brenda. I'm a doctor, Momma."

Speechless, Irene cried tears of joy and sadness at the same time. "I'm proud of you son. You did your sister right by becoming a fancy doctor."

John retrieved the whiskey bottle. "Let's get warm inside the tent and have us a celebration drink or two." He headed into the tent.

Tyrone entered behind John and Irene followed. When she saw the new pillow and fresh pillowcase, she screamed with joy. "If you think I'm gonna go to a White man's hotel with this fine pillow on my bed, you got another thing comin' and won't be so good. Now, where is that whiskey?"

The three sat inside the tent drinking. When the bottle was almost empty, Tyrone fell asleep next to his momma as John stared upward. He tossed one way, then another, fighting his sleep. Around 4:00 am, John grabbed his bag with his clothes, and the money sock he saved his money in and eased out of the tent without even telling them goodbye fearing if he woke Irene, she would convince him to stay. *It's time for me to be a man and make my momma proud.*

John strolled through the camp, taking it in for the last time, not looking back. Not sure of where he was headed as he put one foot in front of the other. It was time to leave Manchester forever. He passed the restaurant. *Thanks for everything.* He kept walking reminiscing about his past in the camp, the hobos he gambled with, and how he received his first pair of shoes that fateful night he met Irene. *Glad you got to see your son.*

6. The Friendly Stranger

ohn walked all day, headed north in a path unknown as to where he'd land. Columbus was the first town he came across. He stopped at a gas station and approached a man who looked like he was fifty years old give or take a year. "What's this town like?"

"Good thing you stopped on this side of the tracks. The other side ain't no kind of nice to Black folks."

"The good Lord has a way of puttin' the right folks in front of me. You suppose there's some kinda of work to be had? I'm a hard worker and need money."

"You must not be from around here, boy, you wandering around asking questions like that can get you in jail or have you working on some White man's plantation."

"Well, I guess I better keep on walking right through this town because I ain't planning on going to jail and I sure ain't working on no White man's plantation."

"I suggest you turn around and head on back wherever you come from. Go back south or head west. If the White folks catch ya on their side of the tracks, you'd be tarred and feathered. Most likely, they'd kill you and take your boots."

"I ain't never been scared of no White man and I ain't about to start now." John's eyes darted over his shoulder as if he expected the White boy's he killed back home to be sneaking up. "How come you ain't in jail or working on no White man's plantation?"

"Because I be the driver for Mr. Lucas, ever heard of him?"

"Nope."

"He be one of the richest men in Muscogee County."

"Oh! So, you don't work on his plantation, you don't even clean up his house, sweep off his porch, or drive his horse and wagon, you drive his car. What that makes you a fancy nigga? Naw, you ain't no field nigga or no porch nigga like your forefathers, hmm you just a dumb nigga. See, your father and your grandfather had to work on the plantation for the master; else they would a got killed or beaten so bad they'd wished they were dead."

"You have some mouth on you, boy for bein' a stranger in these parts."

"I hear ya, but you don't have to and what's so sad is that in your mind, you don't think you do cause you driving a car instead of riding on a horse. Bet that White man ain't never sat up there in that front seat with you and asked you how your day been, boy? How's yo wife and children, boy? Bet if he ever passed out in the back

48

seat of that car and it was you and him, he'd rather die than have your big black lips touch his to blow one breath of that air coming out your lungs. See, you just another nigga to him, nothing special about you to him. If you die today, he'll have em' bring on down the next nigga that know how to drive, and that'll probably be yo son if you got one. I can see you at home now every night making like you teaching him how to drive instead of trying to tell him how to get off that plantation that you work on!"

The man scowled. "Look, boy, I don't know who you are coming in here like you some big shot. You can be no more than fifteen or sixteen, thinking you know so much about life, but don't know nothin' at all. You come through here with everything you own in a croaker sack; you didn't get off no train, just walked up like a thief in the night. So that tells me you ran away from home for whatever reason probably done ran off from master's plantation."

"Listen, I might have come in here like a thief in the night, but I didn't come off no plantation because my daddy was a real man. He raised me to be a man, that's why you see me walking through this town free as a bird to do whatever I want. See, ain't nobody gonna come looking for me, but you see you gotta get on before master sends the folks after you. So, you have yourself a good day and hurry on back. Me, well, imma' headin' on down the road and see what else ya'll got besides plantations and working farms." John strode away headed north against the advice he received.

"Boy, about a half a mile down that ways, you can catch the ferry and go on over to Alabama, Phenix City. You might find that to your liking."

John smiled and kept walking; he didn't even look back. *Alabama here I come, I don't know what you have to offer me, but get ready, cause here I come.* He slowed his gate because he remembered the horror stories about lynching and beating slaves he heard from his mother and father that his grandparents told them. *Negroes aren't that welcomed in Alabama.*

His father's words rang clear. "No matter where you wanna go in this world if you gotta go through Alabama to get there, you best forget about going cause them Satan, himself bred White folk will kill you just cause. White folks don't need no reason."

John stopped and faced the friendly stranger. "Hey, ain't Alabama a bad place for folk like me and you. I mean, least over here in Georgia they let us work, but I heard in Alabama they just like to hunt and kill us."

"Well, I guess that all depends on what part of Alabama your feet land. Right across the river is Phenix City and ain't nothin' going on over there except gambling, bootlegging, and prostituting."

"Sounds like my kind of city. Phenix City, here I come."

"What your name, boy?"

"Pie. That's what my friends call me. My given name is John."

"well, look here Pie, you walked into this town a free man, don't you go over there and get carried out a dead

50

man. Ain't nothing over there, but trouble and trouble is easy to get in, but hard to get out."

"With all due respect, I ain't never been the kind of man went looking for no trouble, but till the day I die, I'm gonna be the kind of man that stands for myself if and when trouble comes my way. I never did get your name."

"That's because I never gave it to you."

They both laughed.

A smile crossed the lips of the stranger. "My name is Jonathan, Jonathan W. Brown."

"Well, Mr. Johnathan W. Brown, it's been nice talking to you, but I better be gettin' along."

"Look, I think you are a very bright young man, and I'd hate to see anything bad happen to you. So, I tell you what, let me pull on down the road a bit, and you come shortly after me, and you can jump in the back and hitch a ride. I'll let you out behind the old sawmill just before the river."

John smiled. "Okay. Probably better that way."

Mr. Brown entered the car and slowly pulled off.

John stood on the side of the road for a few minutes. *What's ahead for me in Phenix City?* He blew air from his lips as he pursed them. *If I get caught, will I get killed? Will I see my next birthday? Will I get married and have a family? Will I find a place to call home? Only God knows.*

7. The River

After daydreaming for a while, allowing Mr. Brown to get on down the road, John picked up his bag and headed north. After an hour, he stopped on the side of the road for a short rest. *Where is he? How far could he have gone? I guess he changed his mind.*

John stood brushing his worn jeans and continued north. When he strode a little further down the road, a small patch of woods came into sight. He shivered. *I don't like no woods. White boys hang there.*

He increased his stride so that he could get past the wooded area. "Psst."

John stopped dead in his tracks as he jerked his head toward the sound. His heart raced as beads of sweat formed on his upper lip.

"Boy, come on over here, so nobody will see you get in the trunk."

John tilted his head toward the ground as he wiped the sweat from his brow and upper lip. "Whew! You scared this Black boy to death." He darted for the brush and toward the car hidden from view. As he approached, a nervous tinge pinched his throat. *Something didn't seem right.* "How come you so far back off in the woods?"

Before Mr. Brown could answer, John remembered the man's words when they first met. *Most wind up in jail or workin' on a White man's plantation. This is a set up if I've ever felt one.*

John's first instinct was to attack, and try to break every bone in his body, or take out his blade, and kill him for even attempting to take him like that and for all the ones that he had probably taken before now. He knew that he couldn't just turn and run.

"You want a ride or not?" Mr. Brown waved for John to get into the truck.

With extreme apprehension and caution, John strode further into the woods just far enough to be out of sight. He glared toward Mr. Brown. "Can you give me a hand with this bag? I have been carrying it a long way for days, and I can't carry it any further." John dropped the bag about one foot in front of him.

Mr. Brown nodded and inched closer to John. "Okay, glad to help." As he strode toward John, he flashed a fake smile. He stopped and bent down as if he was going to tie his shoe. "It sure is cold out here, ain't it?"

"Sure is."

Just as Mr. Brown pick up the croaker sack with John's clothes, John reached into his pocket, grabbed his switchblade, popped it open, and grabbed Mr. Brown around the neck placing the blade at the old man's throat. "Move or make a sound, and I'll kill you right here where you stand. What ya think? I'm some fool? You think I'm just gonna let you take me and make me a slave?"

John punched Mr. Brown in the back of the head as hard as he could jolting the man. The knife almost slit the old man's throat. "Walk over to the car."

Mr. Brown could hardly stand, let alone walk, because John had punched him so hard that he had double-vision for a moment and was dizzy; he couldn't even speak. Still holding the blade around his neck, John reached into Mr. Brown's pocket and pulled out a 22-caliber pistol. He shoved Mr. Brown toward the car.

"Look, boy; please don't kill me, I got a family."

"You got a family! What about my family? You were fixing to try to take me from my family forever. I care nothing about your family, and you don't either because if you did, you wouldn't dare let em' see you doing anything like this to your own people. A real man rather lay down his life and die or hang from a tree with pride. He wouldn't do what you are doing, ain't no telling how many folks you done took from their families and you got the nerve to ask me to spare you for your family. If you cared for your family, you would have taken your family and run off a long time ago, you old fool."

John didn't know if he was more upset at Mr. Brown for trying to kidnap him, or asking him to spare his life for his family's sake when he wasn't considerate of his and ready to take him by force and make him go work on some White man's farm for the rest of his life. "Black folks like you should be hung. You don't do this to your own kind. God show gonna get ya for that."

John put the knife in his pocket but, he pointed the gun right at Mr. Brown's forehead. "You know what? I'm gonna do your family and the world a favor."

Mr. Brown's eyes widened as he swallowed hard. "Please don't kill me. I beg you for my life."

"Oh no! I ain't gonna kill you. I would if I thought God gave some reward for killing the Devil cause you're sure a demon coming straight from the pits of Hell. I bet you are the Devil himself. Naw! I ain't gonna kill you cause you already dead. A man as evil as you gotta be a dead man walking."

Mr. Brown sighed.

John glanced in the opened trunk of the car. Inside a piece of rope caught his eye. "You better not lie to me or I'll kill you where you stand. How far is the river?"

"You can cross over the Thirteenth Street Bridge and enter into Alabama. Maybe about five miles down the road."

"Get in the trunk. That's where you're gonna ride until we cross into Alabama."

"I'll drive you anywhere you wants to go if you don't kill me."

"Get in the trunk, now! Don't make me shoot you when you could live if you do as your told." John waved the gun in his captive's face.

Mr. Brown nodded and climbed into the trunk of the car. John slammed the trunk and got in the car. He drove the car further off into the woods and got out. When he exited, John opened the trunk and glared at the helpless Mr. Brown. "Get out!"

"I thought you said you weren't gonna kill me."

"I said, get out!"

Mr. Brown crawled out of the trunk and waited for further orders.

"Go sit down by that tree and close your eyes." John quickly pointed the gun toward the largest tree. "Don't make a peep or I'll kill you. Understood?"

Mr. Brown nodded his head.

"Good decision. Now go!"

"Please don't shoot me." Mr. Brown stumbled toward the tree. When he reached it, he sat and leaned against it.

"I'm not going to shoot you; I'm gonna tie you up." John kept the gun pointed toward his captive as he dug for the rope. Once he grabbed the rope, he headed toward Mr. Brown. "Don't say one word."

Mr. Brown nodded as John pulled a handkerchief from his back pocket.

John tied the handkerchief around Mr. Brown's mouth to gag him. "That should keep you quiet."

His captive's eyes darted with fear.

After painstakingly securing Mr. Brown to the tree with the rope, he stood over him. "You are as evil, as evil comes. I should kill you, but I'll let the good Lord do with you what He wants. If he wants you to be dead, you'll die against this here tree trunk instead of a good ole fashion hangin' like you should. If it be God's will for you to live, then someone will find you before you take your last breath. Nobody messes with me."

Mr. Brown's eyes teared with fear.

"You're not so brave now that you be in God's hands. Now I suppose that big shot White man will be lookin' for his car. He won't care if you're dead and gone. He'll replace you with your son. I don't want you to tell him bout' me. You hear me? If you do, I'll come back and kill you. But you probably won't see him again anyway."

Mr. Brown nodded in confirmation.

John strolled to the car, and then drove it further down in the woods, got out, and slashed all four tires. He got his sack and a bag of food that Mr. Brown had on the front seat and headed toward the river. He didn't want to walk back toward the road because he wasn't for sure if there were others with Mr. Brown, so he just walked straight ahead and didn't look back.

Before long, darkness fell, and John had been through so much excitement that day that he didn't even realize how cold the ground felt when he lay down to rest. He gazed at the stars. *Mr. Brown deserves everything he has comin. It's justice for all the Black folks he done sold out.*

He attempted to close his eyes to sleep but couldn't because his mind kept wandering. *I can't stay here. I'll get caught.*

He got up, picked up his bags, and headed toward the river. Before long, the bridge peeked in front of him through the tree line. *Almost there.*

John increased his pace. When he made it to the bridge, he stopped and gazed on the sign, which was posted on the state line, "Welcome to Alabama."

"Momma, I made it to Alabama." Tears streamed because there was something inside that told him he would never return Georgia, which meant he never would see his mother's face or hear her sweet voice or his family again. He took his first step in Alabama.

8. The Ride

J ohn felt like an older man who had lived out his life through its entirety, and he was about to die as he eased his second step onto the bridge on his way into Alabama. *A myriad of things kept his mind busy. Is my family looking for me? Did they hear what happened? Did the police question them? Did the White folks come after them? Was the Ku Klux Klan harassing anyone related to me? Had they hung my family for not knowing where I was?*

"I did what I did to defend myself. I'm not a murderer. *God won't let anything happen to my family.*

John wrapped his coat tight around him, pulled his cap down over his ears, and raced across the bridge. Although it was a short distance, it seemed to be miles to John because part of him wanted to escape the bad luck he had faced in Georgia, but the other part desired to sprint back to Georgia, return home, face his punishment, which surely would be death, and see his family one more time. John stopped midway across the bridge and looked down at the water for a moment. A truck pulled onto the bridge. The truck slowed, and John immediately had a flashback of why he had even left Macon. *Okay, this is how I'm going to die by freezing or drowning because I'm not getting dragged off by some White men and killed.*

Just as John was about to put his foot upon the rail to jump off the bridge, the truck came to a screeching halt. "Hey what are you doing out here this time of night by yourself, boy?"

John could tell by the sound of the voice that it wasn't a White man, so he took his foot down and turned around and faced an older Black man and a Black soldier.

The older gentlemen nodded. "Get in."

John remembered what Mr. Brown had tried to do, and he vowed to never trust anyone after that. "If it's all right with ya'll, I'll jump on the back."

The driver smiled and nodded. "Well, jump on."

John jumped in the back of the truck. *As soon as this truck slows or makes the first stop, I'm jumping off and running. No White man is ever gonna get me.* One thing John learned earlier that day from Mr. Brown was evil comes in all shapes and colors; and no discrimination. He didn't care that one of the men was a soldier, he planned to jump off.

Once over the bridge and about five miles down the road, the soldier leaned his head out the window. "Where are you going?

"Right here will be fine, you can let me off."

The driver eased the truck over to the side of the road and stopped. John quickly jumped off of the truck clutching his belonging and immediately ran to the other side of the road to put some distance between him and the men.

The soldier frowned. "You're welcome."

John stopped and turned to the soldier. "Thank you very much."

"My name is Ralph, and this is my father, Jimmy, we not gonna hurt you. You can come back over here and talk to us."

Something about these two men gave John a sense of security along with relief, and because he had the pistol, he stole from Mr. Brown in his pocket, and he wasn't scared to use it, he strode back to the truck. "I'm sorry for that. It's not that I don't like your kindness, but I got in a bit a trouble earlier in the day when a Black man tried to kidnap me for his White man he drives for. I gotta be safe. You ever heard of a Mr. Brown?"

Jimmy nodded and touched his chest above his heart. "I heard of men taking strange boys who come into town, making them work their farms, and whatnot, for many years till they were too old to work, and when they let em' go, they would be so old, they would have forgotten why they came and what they were looking for."

"That's what I'm runnin' from. I was lucky I got away from him out there in the woods. That's where he planned on trapping me, but I outsmarted him."

"Boy, you one lucky Black man. Our kind don't escape often."

John drew in a deep breath. "I'm cold, is your offer for a ride still good?"

"Get in."

The men laughed, and John entered the truck as the soldier inched to the center to make room.

John slammed the truck door. "All in."

Jimmy pressed the accelerator and eased down the road headed north. "Where you headin' boy?"

"Not really sure. Just headed north to get out of the south. I heard the north treat Black folk better."

"I heard the same thing." Ralph flashed a smile. "I've been there. They do treat Black folk better."

John yawned. "You mind if I get me a wink of shut eye?"

"Go ahead. I'll wake you when we turn off onto our road."

Several hours had elapsed as the truck headed north. The truck slowed, turned left, and several hundred yards in front stood a shack. The driver eased his foot from the accelerator and pressed the brake bringing the truck to a stop. "Wake him, Son."

Ralph shook John. "This is where we part ways."

John opened his eyes and looked around. "Where is here?"

Jimmy tapped the steering wheel. "Up ahead is my house. Why don't you come on in and spend the night with us? Ain't no sense in a young man waking up on Christmas morning all by himself?"

John had been through so much that he didn't even realize it was Christmas Eve. "Sounds good to me. I can't even remember the last time I been inside of a house, much less for Christmas."

"I take that as a yes." Jimmy pressed the accelerator and eased up to the house.

The three exited the vehicle and headed inside.

When they stepped in, a woman ran up to Ralph and embraced him. "My baby done come home for Christmas."

"Momma, it's good to be home." Ralph kissed her on the cheek.

Jimmy cleared his throat. "Where's your manners boy? Introduce our company."

"I'm sorry, Momma. This is John, a... a friend of mine. John, this is my momma, Miss Rosie."

John extended his hand. "It's a pleasure to meet you, ma'am."

"Momma, I brought you a present."

"You didn't have to do that."

"The way things are smellin' in here, I'd say I do. What you got in the oven?" Ralph pulled a wrapped present from his bag and handed it his momma. "Go ahead, open it."

Rosie slowly opened the gift cherishing every moment. When she lifted the last flap, a beautiful crisp new apron lay in the box. She immediately put it on. "I love it. Dinner is almost ready. I just need to set another place for our guest. Ya'll go ahead and get to the table."

"I love you, momma, and I've missed you so much."

"I said, get to the table."

9. The Supper

John, as a guest of the Christmas Eve dinner, sat opposite of Ralph. Rosie and Jimmy sat at each end of the table which had enough food displayed; it looked as if they were expecting a dozen more guests. Rosie extended both hands palms up. "Let's bless this food."

Everyone held hands as they bowed their heads. An uncomfortable silence befell the room. Rosie cleared her throat. "Where's your manners, Ralph? You've forgottin' how to pray while you was away?"

"No, mamma. I was waitin' to hear yours. It's been a long time."

Rosie pursed her lips as she squeezed Ralph's hand. "Dear Lord, thank you for bringin' my Ralph back to us in one piece. Thank you for your Son that gave his life to us so that we may have eternal life with you. Bless John through his travels and may he reach wherever, his road leads, he does so in Your grace. Bless this food that nourishes our body. Amen."

"Amen!" John grinned. "I haven't heard a momma's prayer in a long time. Thank you for that."

She gazed into John's eyes as she handed him the mashed potatoes. "What brings you into these parts without your momma or daddy?"

"It's a long story I'd rather not tell over a good supper like this." He placed a spoonful of potatoes on his plate and passed them to Jimmy.

"Okay, then. What are your plans?" She put a piece of turkey on his plate. "Gravy?"

"Yes, gravy."

She covered the turkey with gravy and added the stuffing. "Again, what are your plans?"

They continued to pass the bowls of food as they filled their plates.

"I want to find a nice quiet town where us Black folks are treated fair, get a job and save up enough money, so I can go up north and make a life for myself."

Jimmy swallowed a bite of peas. "Sounds like you have it thought out."

"Not enough. I need a job so I can get out of here. I don't want to spend all my life in the south working for peanuts or on some White man's plantation. As soon as I'm established in the north, I'm coming back to Georgia for my family."

Rosie grinned. "Well, you ain't going up north tonight, so you might as well get comfortable. It's Christmas eve, and the weather gonna get bad."

Ralph smiled. "It looks like my momma likes you. She don't invite strange folk to spend the night."

"That's right. When bedtime comes, I'll make you a bed on the couch in front of the fire."

"I can't tell you the last time I slept with a roof over my head. That is besides a tent roof."

Jimmy wiped his mouth with his napkin. "It's been rough for you being so young I would imagine."

"It won't always be this way. I will make it north and make my momma proud."

"I get it." Jimmy nodded. "When I was about your age, I worked hard and saved every penny to buy some land. I own this house and the property. You can do it if you put your mind to it."

"Oh, I made up my mind a long time ago when I high-tailed out on the first freight train."

"What about schooling?" Jimmy took a bite of his turkey.

"I made it to the eighth grade. I reckon I don't need no more to get ahead. I can count mighty fine."

"I wanted Ralph to get his college education. That's how us Black folks can get ahead."

"I wanted to go into the Army."

"Son, yes, you did. Your heart was set on joining the White man's army, and I let you, but your education is still important."

"I can't thank you good folks enough for bringin' me into your home. I feel like I'm with family, again. I wish I'd never had to leave my family."

Jimmy's brow furrowed. "What do you mean, had to leave?"

"Things got out of control one night. I was attacked by two White boys and during the struggle I accidently killed them. I was only taking up for myself, but I ran knowing that the White folk would kill me."

John recanted the entire story from start to finish. "I'm not sorry for killing those boys because they robbed me from being with my family."

Rosie shoved her plate forward. "Hush! I don't want to hear another word about it. God was with you that night and don't you ever forget it. You probably saved another Black child from a worse fate."

"I do feel guilty sometimes and I'm afraid God is gonna send me straight to Hell."

"Don't you worry about that." Rosie smiled. "You did the right thing. Ask God to forgive you and head north as soon as you can. And, you don't be worrin' about your family. God will take care of them too."

Jimmy stretched and yawned. "My belly is so full. Thank you, Rosie, it was delicious. I'm callin' it a night."

"Thank you, Mr. Jimmy, for brinin' me here."

"Your welcome. Just stay out of trouble."

Rosie glanced at her son. "Ralph, clear the table, and I'll get the linens and make John's bed."

"You don't have to do that. If you bring me the covers, I can make it myself."

"Very well. It'll be nice to have someone sleep on the couch again. That was my brother's bed until he died a few years back. I'll get the bedding; you help Ralph clear the table."

"With pleasure. Thank you again for such a fine meal."

With his belly full, it didn't take John five minutes to fall asleep. Early the next morning before John opened his eyes and was still half asleep; he was hit in the nose by a familiar scent the smell of grits, country ham, eggs, and biscuits. He got up and folded the bedding. Then headed toward the kitchen.

"John, you up. Is that you, we hear stirring?" Rosie's voice drifted from the kitchen.

John entering the kitchen said, "I can't thank you and Mr. Jimmy enough for letting me sleep here last night."

"No thanks needed. Go sit down and get you some breakfast. The others are on their way. They're just finishing up with some outside chores."

"No, thank you. You've been more than generous to me. My momma always said not to overstay your welcome when it comes your way."

The back door opened, and Jimmy and Ralph entered.

"That's nonsense."

Jimmy's brow creased.

"What nonsense?" Rosie said.

"John here don't think he needs a good breakfast. He's afraid he'll overstay his welcome."

"Boy, sit down and eat. You don't know where your next meal will come from. Besides, what are you leaving for in such a hurry. North will wait on you."

"I got to find a job."

"Not on Christmas day. Besides, we need help around here with Ralph in the Army, and his uncle passing. I can't pay you, but I can give you room and board and three good meals a day."

That was like music to John's ears because he didn't have anywhere else to go, and he didn't mind working. Plus, he wasn't worried about money because he knew he would be able to knock a hustle and get some cash; plus, he had about sixty-five dollars that he had saved from working at the restaurant and gambling with the hobos. "You've got yourself a hired hand."

Rosie nodded and smiled as she handed John his breakfast. "Glad you're stayin' around. Now eat, there's more chores to be done."

John laughed as he sat down. Ralph sat across from him. "As soon as I report back to duty, you can bunk in my bed. I'm glad you're stayin' around here. My parents need a strong handyman."

10. The Suit

Winter soon departed as the ground thawed easing into spring. For the first time, John cherished the fruit tree blossoms and the flower beds as the dead foliage turned vibrant green and color bloomed; his favorite, the yellow daffodils because they reminded him of his mother. When he was eight, he always made sure he picked the wild ones for her so she would have a fresh bouquet.

He worked hard into the hot humid summer, through the fall, and before he knew it, winter was upon him again. His stay with Jimmy and Rosie seemed a natural fit, and he had grown to love them as his family and was grateful they took him into their home. He had found his favorite thing, a gambling house, and little by little, he saved his gambling money in the sock he hid beneath Ralph's bed never giving up on his dream of going north.

JESSICA SIMS

One morning, John woke up to the sweet aroma of a peach pie. It smelled just like the ones his mother used to bake. He jumped up, got dressed, and raced to the kitchen where Rosie pulled a cobbler out of the oven. "Ms. Rosie, what's the occasion?"

"I baked this pie for a special young man; today is his birthday."

At that moment, John realized that it was him; he was the birthday boy. John had turned seventeen, and he had been gone from home for more than a year. "Hey, it's my birthday."

"Yes, it is."

Jimmy entered the house through the back door. "Happy birthday, boy."

"Thank you." John pondered for a minute. "How did y'all know it was my birthday?"

Jimmy and Rosie laughed. Rosie gave John a hug. "You do a lot of talking in that bed at night, and one thing you always say is October twenty-third. I figured that must be a special day for you. Since you don't have a wife, I know it's not your anniversary, and you don't have no kids, so it can't be one of your children's birthday; so, it must be yours."

"I often dream of spending time with my momma and her teaching me my birthday at five. I guess I talk in my sleep. Never been accused of that before."

Rosie tapped John's shoulder. "You just sit yourself down here because we got something for you."

John scrapped the chair's legs across the floor and quickly sat. Rosie handed a box wrapped in a brown paper bag.

"You didn't have to buy me nothin' to make me happy. You do so much for me already."

"Don't worry about that; just open your gift."

John tore the paper, opened the box, and inside was a beautiful brass pocket watch. "I don't know what to say. This is the best gift I've ever received. Thank you, both."

Jimmy smiled. "You know what time it is?"

John looked at his pocket watch. "It's six thirty-two."

"That might be right, but it's time for us to get into the field before it gets too late."

Rosie held up her hand. "Hold on; I got something else." She reached into the cabinet, pulled out a large flat box and handed it to John.

He gazed at the package read the label. "It's from Ralph. He's in New Jersey."

He opened the box and there it was, a brand-new suit. "A suit! Not just any suit, a suit straight from the city. It's the kind like Irene's son had on when he got off the bus that day."

"You got your money for goin' up north?" Jimmy pursed his lips.

"Not yet; but I don't care. This is the best birthday I have ever had."

11. The First Love

ohn worked for two years for his room and board. Jimmy and Rosie became more like his parents, than a couple he luckily found. Well-known by the locals, and well-loved, he fit in for the first time in his life. Troubles of his past seemed to fade as better memories formed. His money sock became two as he gambled at night. It might not be the living his momma back home would have wanted, but he was safe and had a roof over his head. His dream of going north didn't seem as strong.

The sun set over the back porch as Rosie stepped out. "John, can you come help me please?"

He bolted from around the corner covered in grease. "You need me?"

"I sure do, honey. The sun's going down. Get yourself cleaned up and get in the house."

"I'll be here in about five minutes."

"Boy, you better make it three."

John raced to the side of the house straight to Jimmy's truck. He grabbed several tools and then slammed the hood. Jimmy came from the front of the house.

"You got ole Bessy runnin' yet?"

"Not yet. Real soon though."

"Good, we can't run this place without it."

"One day when I go north and become rich, I'm gonna buy you a new one."

"I'll hold you to that. When you think you'll be heading that way?"

"I'm not sure. Mr. Jimmy, right now I'd better get myself inside and see what Ms. Rosie wants. I can't thank you enough for everything you and the misses have done for me."

"God sent you to me because my Ralph doesn't want to stay around here. He knew we couldn't do it by ourselves, so he sent you to take his place."

Rosie came from around the corner. "I told both of you to get cleaned up."

"Sorry, Ms. Rosie." John wiped his hands on an old greasy rag.

"Meet me on the front porch. I want to talk to you about something serious. Now hurry." She strode toward the front porch and sat down on the swing. She grabbed her crochet from a basket at her feet and then busied her fingers creating a blanket.

John rounded the corner and ran straight to the porch. Once there, he leaned against the column and winked at Rosie. "I'm here. What's so important I couldn't finish fixing the truck."

"You know what tomorrow is?"

"Sure do, you make me peach pie."

"No! It's the Lord's day."

"Lord's day?"

"The day you take time to be with the Lord."

"My momma always said I was always with the Lord."

"This is the day you do for the Lord. You're going to church with me in the morning. I wouldn't be a good momma if I didn't make you go to church."

"You sound just like my momma. She made me go to church too."

"When was the last time you stepped into God's house?"

"The week before I had to leave home."

"Then, it's about time. You can wear that city slicker suit and get all fancied up. Give the girls something to croon about."

"Go get cleaned up and get that grease out of your nails. Don't you go embarrassing me."

"I won't Ms. Rosie, I promise. I owe you that much."

"Boy, you owe me nothin' but respect. Now get!"
***

The next morning as the sun sifted between the curtain waking John. He yawned, stretched, and then bolted upright. He grabbed his pocket watch and looked at the time. His eyes darted to his city slicker suit.

Downstairs, Rosie, dressed in her Sunday's best, sat the third plate down onto the breakfast table as Jimmy took his first bite. "He's cuttin' it close."

"Don't worry yourself, Rosie. John's a man of his word. He'll be dressed and ready to go. You watch and see."

Rosie sat and took a bite of her biscuit covered by white gravy.

Before she could swallow, John stood in the doorway dressed to the tee in his city slicker suit and leather shoes he saved up to buy. "How do I look?"

Rosie gave him the once over. "You look like one of those city boys, you clean up mighty fine."

"Jimmy, do I have your approval."

"Let me see. Something's missing. I can't put my finger on it."

John reached into his pocket and retrieved his pocket watch. "I would never forget. How could I?"

"Like the misses said, you look mighty fine. You watch those young ladies turn their heads at church today."

The three of them drove toward the white church in the foreground; they pulled in and parked. After they exited the truck, they entered toward the front door.

A group of teenage girls dressed in their Sunday best, giggled as John passed their way. Loretta, a beautiful dark-skinned young lady, with chestnut eyes, long black hair like silk, and a body shaped like an hourglass flashed him a wide grin, waved, and quickly diverted her eyes to her friends. "He's so handsome."

Thankful they couldn't tell how embarrassed he became, John, strode quickly toward the pastor.

The pastor first shook Jimmy's hand. "Glad to see you and the misses."

"It's always good to be seen."

Irene extended her hand. "I brought you a peach pie for later."

"I can taste it now. The good Lord, do provideth."

John stepped forward. "Good to see you, Pastor."

"Same here, John. It's been way too long since you graced God's house."

Rosie nudged John on his arm. "I told you."

"Today's sermon will be perfect for you, John. It's how to make a plan under the arms of God's will."

"I'll be sure to listen. I got me some plans to go north. That is, if it's God's plan for me." John glanced toward Lorretta and flashed a smile.

"Never underestimate what God has in store for you."

"No, Pastor, I'd never."

Rosie giggled. "I see you got your eyes on Lorretta."

Bashful from the comment, John pursed his lips and entered the church.

***

One month passed, and John chased Loretta like a hound on a squirrel. He wasn't going to give up until she gave in. Loretta played hard to get although she was attracted to John. She learned the dating game from her three older sisters and the game of cat and mouse. Eventually, she gave in, and the two dated.

FINDING HOME

John wasn't in love with Loretta, but he enjoyed spending time with her, and she enjoyed spending time with him, and Sunday's was their day. John visited Loretta at her parents' house for dinner after church, or she went to see Ms. Rosie and Mr. Jimmy.

Loretta's parents liked John because he was hardworking, and he often worked for her father to help him out when in a bind. John became a talented handyman because he knew how to fix just about anything.

Before long, John's thoughts of home were few and far in between. He settled in Phenix city, Alabama. However, deep down, he felt that this place was like Manchester, Georgia, only a pit stop. Something inside of him told him that he needed to do more with his life. Although life treated John well in Phenix city, he didn't feel he could call it home.

One fateful Sunday, on a walk hand-in-hand, Loretta and John seemed at peace and in love. Loretta squeezed his hand. "I've got something on my mind I need to tell you."

He smiled. "You can tell me anything."

"I'm moving out of Phenix City."

John tugged at her hand and stopped. He faced her with a scowl. "What do you mean, moving out of Phenix City? Where you going?"

"To the big city of New York. My older sister took a job there and my family doesn't want her to go alone."

"I know we're not serious about each other, but I don't want you to go."

"You heard Ms. Rosie tell me that if I stay here, I'd wind up cleaning up for some White woman. That's not the life I want. I want a better life."

"I don't like this at all."

"It's a big world out there and I want to see it."

John shook his head. *Now, I'm glad I never asked her to marry me.* He gave her a gentle-heartbroken smile.

"There is one thing that would make me stay."

"What's that."

She held out her hand and wiggled her wedding band finger. "An engagement."

John took a deep breath as he stared at the ground. "Loretta, you're a wonderful girl and deserve the best."

She flashed a huge, anticipatory grin.

"You deserve somebody better than me because I'm not good enough. I don't have nothin' I can offer a fine young lady like yourself."

Tears welled in Loretta's eyes. "John, you are good enough."

"I don't have a job. I can barely take care of myself. How am I supposed to take care of a wife?"

"It's not about what you have; it's whether you love me."

The still silence grew as John gently wiped her tears from both cheeks. "If you love someone and they want to leave, be it leaving town or leaving you, let them go, and if it's meant to be, they'll come back."

"You know you don't believe that."

"I do mean it. Please don't make this any harder than it needs to be. It's not that I don't love you, I don't even know if I love myself. I'm not good for nobody's husband."

"Then it's settled; I'll be leaving Saturday morning."

"I'm not gonna lie. I'm gonna miss you, and I'll never forget your kindness and all you have done for me."

The walk back to Loretta's house, was met with silence and tears until Loretta finally got the courage to speak. "I have one month until I graduate. I'll continue to teach you what I learn in school."

"That's mighty kind of you. One day, when I find myself, I'm coming after you and I'll make you the happiest woman alive."

***

One month later, Loretta graduated from high school and left for New York City on a bus. That day as the bus pulled away, John waved. *I will find you if it's in God's plan. Just like Pastor said.*

He ran behind the bus as Loretta gazed out the window with tears rolling down her face until it was out of sight.

John felt as if his heart stopped beating, and everything was in slow motion. After a minute, he strode home with a heavy heart. The same heavy heart that he had the day he hopped on the train leaving everyone and everything behind. He passed the old mulberry tree where he and Loretta sat in the evenings while she taught him what she learned in school that day. He sat beneath the tree. *Why me, Lord? I should've asked her to marry me.*

He leaned against the tree trunk, closed his eyes, and fell asleep. He must have slept for about two hours before he woke up and headed home.

When he entered through the back door, Rosie smiled and nodded. "How about a piece of peach pie?"

"I don't feel like eating."

"Heartbreak will do that sort of thing to a man. Sounds like you got it bad."

"I never even got to say a real goodbye to Loretta. By the time I got to the station, she was already on the bus and it pulled away."

She placed her warm hand on his shoulder. "If it's meant to be or in God's plan for the both of you to be together, then she will either come back, or the good Lord will send you to where she is, either way, the both of you will be reunited."

"Loretta was the one reason I stayed here in Phenix City. Not much left for me to hang around no more. I feel empty inside. I don't have my family and now I don't have my Loretta."

"Everything will work out. You wait and see. Trust in the good Lord."

"You know maybe there is a curse on my life. I have never gone looking for trouble, but trouble always seems to find me. The last time I remember being happy was when I was five and got my first pair of new shoes; not a pair my brothers handed down to me, but a pair my mother got from the White woman she worked for."

"You listen to me because I speak the truth. There's no curse on your life. God has a hand on it. He's protecting you. If He weren't, you'd be a dead man by now."

"I suppose, those White boys tried to kill me, someone tried to kidnap me, and I've been in a lot of fights where I could have died."

"Your somebody special to God. He has a plan for you and a calling on your life."

"If you say so."

"Boy, hold your head up. What you need to do is to start working to find out what that calling is and what the Lord wants you to do. Until you do that son, nothing is gonna seem right and you gonna always have that empty feeling inside."

12. The Millworker

John lay in his bed as the moon shimmered through the curtains. *I guess my time is up here.* Loretta was the main reason that he had stayed in Phenix City for so long and that the city had some of the biggest gambling houses he had ever seen. After his first love left, he often gambled and won big too. Like always, he didn't mind letting anybody know that he didn't play with his money and it didn't take the locals long to learn that he had a blade and a gun, and he didn't mind using either.

One night, not long after Loretta left, John entered a poker game. Two bystanders, who stood in the corner, took notice of his winnings. They had watched him win money for about two weeks, so they decided to steal from him. They knew that John always drank moonshine after he left the gambling game, and tonight was no different. He'd won about forty bucks, decided he was done, got him a drink, and left out the back.

The two men followed behind.

John increased his pace as he headed toward the trail to his home. He knew the men were following him, so he pretended to be drunker than Cooter Brown staggering and mumbling to himself.

The two men were right behind him, and when they were far enough into the woods, they ran up to John, one from the back, and another from the front.

John was ready with his gun in his hand and pulled the trigger, firing a warning shot.

The thug in the back tried to grab John, but before he did, John pointed the gun at him. "Touch me, and I'll kill you, and then, him. Now get on out of here."

The man in the front took off and ran.

With his gun still pointed at the other man's head, he waved it. "I should just kill you."

The man slowly turned as John reached into his pocket and retrieved a couple of dollars from him. Then, he hit him on the back of the head with the gun. "I would take that shirt you got on, but you've got blood all over it, so it won't do me no good." He tossed the bills onto the man's back.

John strode quickly home. *Now what? Do I go or do I stay?*

It didn't take long for the story to get out about John and the would-be robbers, and from then on, nobody else tried to rob John no matter how drunk he was when he left the gambling house.

A few days later, John ran some errands for Mr. Jimmy. He stopped by the general store to pick up some items for Ms. Rosie. Once he entered the store, his heart started beating fast, beads of sweat formed on his brow and upper lip, and his eyes got bigger and brighter than the sun on a hot summer day. He swallowed hard trying to rid the lump in his throat which formed. "I don't believe it. Willie Chambless, is that really you?"

"Here in the flesh. How you been, cuz?"

John just stood there in disbelief. "Mercy me; my eyes must be fooling me, Lord. Junior, is that really you?"

The two walked toward each other and embraced.

"Have you lost your mind, John? What caused you to leave home and your mamma like that?"

"It's a long story I'm tryin' to forget."

"Your momma thinks you're dead and your daddy thinks you got killed by the Klu Klux Klan. Is you done gone crazy or something?"

"No, I'm still Pie, and still in my right mind. I probably have gained a little more sense since I left."

"My, my. I forgot about that nickname of yours. Pie, you still eat it?"

"What do you think?"

"You got a misses who bakes?"

John shook his head with a frown.

Junior punched John on the shoulder. "Why in the world did you walk off from home like that? Just disappeared without a trace."

"A man gotta be a man; can't live off mamma and pappa forever. What brings you to Phenix City? You're a long ways from home."

"Work. A sawmill. I've been there for about a year."

"You a millworker?"

"Naw, man. I help set up the mills and get them running."

"You're a big shot. Where you staying at?"

"The White folks I'm with are staying at a hotel, and the rest of us sleep in the back of the trucks. You got a home of your own I can sleep at while I'm here?"

"I have a room. I work for a couple for my room and board. I do handyman things for them. They are a great couple and treat me like family. In a way, like parents do."

"Sounds like you're making out all right."

"How's my momma, pappa, and the rest of my family?"

Junior's brow furrowed as he took a deep breath. "Your daddy died last year. He got sick the winter before and never could get over it. One day, he never woke up. It crushed you momma, and she's not been the same since."

John just stood there for a moment and visualized what seemed to be every day and every moment that he had spent with his father throughout his life. He didn't want to break down in front of Junior, so he held his tears and changed the subject. "Where you building this sawmill at?"

"Off of Brickyard Road."

Meet me right here around seven. I'll come later after my errands and chores are done. I got us a real nice gambling spot if you're still into that kind of thing. Women will be there too."

"You bet I am."

***

On the way home, it was a bitter-sweet moment because John was happy to see his cousin, but he was depressed about the news of his father. When he arrived, he opened the back door to a fresh baked cherry pie that Ms. Rosie pulled from the oven. She giggled. "You're like a clock. The minute my pie is ready, you come through that door."

John nodded and slumped his shoulders.

"What's wrong with you? You still have Loretta on your mind?"

"Not this time, Ms. Rosie. I ran into one of my cousins at the general store. He told me my pappa passed."

"That was God putting your cousin in your path. Just think if you had waited five minutes or gone to the store five minutes earlier, you would have missed him, but God had it planned for you to be in that store at that exact moment and your cousin too."

"I don't really care. I should've been there for my momma."

"It's a blessing. God showed you exactly what you needed to know."

John wiped a tear. "You know what, you right. In fact, you're always right and you always know what to say to make me feel better. So, maybe God sent me to you, so that you could make me see things the Godly way like my momma."

Ms. Rosie smiled. "You better go finish up out back. Jimmy is having a hard time today. He could use a second pair of hands."

"Yes, ma'am. Maybe work is what I need to get my mind off things back home."

"Son, you are home."

John went out back to the shed and finished working on some things for Mr. Jimmy; he could hardly function thinking about his cousin and the excitement of meeting up with him later. The aroma of Rosie's chicken and dumplings drifted from the house; his stomach growled. He finished up, went inside, and washed his hands for dinner.

The three sat and ate their supper.

John rubbed his stomach. "Ms. Rosie, that was as good as always. Maybe even better. I'm stuffed."

Jimmy swallowed his last bite. "I agree. These dumplings are better than usual. You must have something special in them."

"You two stop it. Dumplings are dumplings. Just be thankful the good Lord sees fit that we have enough to eat."

John sipped his tea. "I'm meeting up with my cousin tonight. I want to catch up with everything that's been going on back home."

Jimmy pursed his lips. "Sounds like a wise choice as long as you stay out of trouble."

"Why don't you bring him over for dinner tomorrow." Rosie sipped her tea. "I bet he'd like a good home cooked meal. Besides, if he's your family, he's our family."

"That's music to my ears. I want you both to meet him and for him to see where I live. Right now, he's sleeping in the back of a truck. You mind if I invite him to sleep in the shed?"

Rosie stood as she picked up John's plate. "No family sleeps in no shed. He can bunk on the couch like you did when you first arrived."

"Thank you. You both are very kind. May I be dismissed? I want get all cleaned up and impress Junior with my city slicker suit."

She nodded. "Go on. It'll do you some good to get your mind off things."

John helped clear the table.

Rosie took a deep breath. "No need to help with the dishes tonight. Go on, go meet your cousin."

"Thanks, Ms. Rosie." John bolted to his bedroom, quickly cleaned up and put on his suit. He admired his reflection in the cracked mirror. *I haven't worn this since taking Loretta to the church picnic.*

John got all fresh and headed out the door more excited than when he would be going to go on a Sunday drive with Loretta. When he arrived at the front of the general store, Junior was waiting along with five others. Junior extended his hand. "Good to see you, Pie."

John glanced at the five men. "Wait, how come I don't know none of ya'll if ya'll are from Monroe county?"

89

Junior put his arm around John. "They aren't from Monroe County. They're from Atlanta. That's where I met them."

"That's a relief. I don't like to meet nobody from Monroe County. Don't know what they know about me. I gotta be careful."

"Don't trouble your mind. These are good folk. I trust them. Now where's that gambling spot of yours and bring on the women too. That's why we're all here."

John led the way to the gambling hall. Before long, he and the others were in with the flow of things at the spot drinking whiskey and flirting with the ladies.

John did what he always did and ordered a toddy and jumped right into a game of craps. To him, that was the easiest way to make a dime.

Time passed; John forgot about his cousin and the five men he escorted to the club. He won about a hundred dollars and he felt fine.

Junior came from across the room and kneeled by him. "Why did you do it, man?"

"Shhh. Don't be talkin about the White boys in here. You want us killed?"

"No, why did you leave home and not tell anybody?"

John picked up his winnings. "Let's take this outside."

The two exited through the back door. When they got outside, John sat on a large rock and gazed up at Junior. "Do you remember the two White boys killed in the woods the night I left town?"

Junior glared at John. "They haven't found out who done it, yet. You killed those White boys and ran. Didn't you?"

"I didn't do it, but I saw who did. I got scared and ran. I thought they'd kill me too. So, I hopped the train as fast as I could and got away."

"You been in Phenix City all this time?"

"No, I had a layover in Manchester Georgia. An older woman, kinda like my mamma took me in."

"Nice house?"

"A tent. We lived in a hobo camp."

"People back home think whoever killed those White boys ran up north. A lot of folks moved away that year because the Ku Klux Klan got out of control. They were out for revenge. They rode just about every night for nine months. Every Black person in town was guilty to them White folk. Blacks were hung or coming up missing and being found in the river almost every day."

"Sounds like I did the right thing jumpin' that train." *I can't trust him with the truth.*

"Nobody ever thought you did it."

Junior was about six years older than John, and deep down he knew John refrained from telling him the truth. "Don't go back to Monroe County."

"Don't plan on it. Remember those good folks I live with? Miss Rosie invited you for supper tomorrow night. She said you can sleep on the couch.

"Sounds like a fine time. How do I get there?"

"No mind yourself with that. Meet me in front of the general store at five and I'll take you there myself."

FINDING HOME

***

The next night, John introduced Junior to Jimmy and Rosie. When junior saw Ms. Rosie, he flashed a grin. "I see why you been here so long, she looks just like your momma, and he talks just like your daddy."

Rosie pointed to the dining table. "Supper is ready. You boys are just in time. Have a seat."

John led the way. He sat in his usual spot and pointed to the vacant chair across from him. "You can sit in Ralph's spot."

"Ralph?" Puzzlement crossed Junior's brow.

"Ralph is their son who is off in the Army. I sleep in his room."

Everyone took a seat except Rosie who put food on everyone's plate.

Junior nodded. "Thank you both very much for the invite. It's been a long time since I had a home cooked meal."

"You're just like family." Rosie placed a spoonful of fried okra on Junior's plate.

"How much longer do you plan on staying here with these fine folks?" Junior stared at John as if to say it was time to leave and head north.

"A bit longer. I'm saving my money. When I have enough, I'm headin' north."

"If you want to earn some more money, we need help at the sawmill. I can get you a job. When we're finished here, we're heading to Montgomery, Alabama. There's plenty of work to be had."

"I'll think about it."

Rosie smiled. "What's there to think about. A paying job? Besides, Ralph comes home next week and will be needing his bed."

"Junior, it looks like I'll be working at that sawmill and go with you to Montgomery."

Jimmy sipped his tea. "You're doing the right thing, John. We'll miss you around here, but it's time for you to get a real job."

A tear fell down Rosie's cheek. "You can always come back here if things don't work out."

"I'll come back and visit on holidays."

"You better or you'll be in a whole lot of trouble. What are you boy's plans for after dinner?"

John shrugged his shoulders. "I'm mighty tired. I'm calling it a quick night and off to bed." John stood.

"Wait!" Junior rose. "Thanks for the supper. I'm going to spend time with my cousin."

John and Junior left the table and went straight to John's room.

Junior looked around. "Not bad. You got lucky. It must be your gambling luck."

"I work for this bed."

"I don't mean nothin' by it. Look, let's go out tonight and try out some of that gambling luck of yours."

"I don't wanna go anywhere tonight. Let's just stay here; I got some whiskey. We can just sit outside with old Mr. Jimmy and talk. He's something else when he gets his head bad."

"Naw man, let's go to the spot, I wanna have some fun, it's my last weekend here in Phenix city; besides I met a girl over there I gotta see one last time."

"I get it. Give me a minute, and I'll meet you at the front door."

Junior nodded and left the room. John dug for his money sock and counted every penny, nickel, dime, quarter, and dollar surprised at how much he managed to save and not gambled away.

***

John and Junior headed to the gambling club. When they arrived, it was already jumping with people having a good time, the music played loud, the girls flirted, and the crap game was wide open.

Junior found Sadie, the girl who attracted him. She was a regular and also had a man. In fact, she had beaus, but one, in particular, Buster was his name, happened to be one of the boys who tried to rob John was very much in love with Sadie and would get angry with any man who spoke to her. When he saw Sadie and Junior dancing, his anger flared. He grabbed Sadie's arm. "I don't know who this boy is, but you belong to me."

Junior wasn't by any means a coward. "I don't see any stamp on Sadie's head saying she belongs to you. Why don't you find someone else to bother? The lady wants to dance with me."

Infuriated, Buster punched Junior in the face, and a brawl broke out.

John bolted to the aid of his cousin and tried to break up the fight.

Buster pulled out his blade to slice Junior; however, John grabbed Buster's hand, stopping him. "You cut him, and I'll kill you."

John snatched the blade out of Buster's hand and gave it to Junior. "Put it in your pocket. You might need it one day."

The other people laughed at Buster as he stormed out.

John nudged Junior. "You okay?"

"Better than fine whiskey."

"You need to watch yourself. Buster is a sneaky man. He tried to rob me once. Didn't get too far when I put a gun to his head."

"You know me, as long as a man's heart is pumping blood just like mine, he doesn't scare me at all, but if it's pumping anything else, he might scare me."

"You still need to watch your back. Look, I'm tired. You coming with me?"

"You go ahead. I know where I'm laying my head tonight."

"Be careful."

"I'm a big boy. I can take care of myself."

"I'll come by the mill tomorrow. Later." John left out the door and headed toward home.

Junior strolled over to Sadie and grabbed her by the hand. "Now, where were we?"

"You sure you wanna start where we left off?"

"Naw. Actually, I don't." He tugged her hand and led her to her upstairs bedroom.

Just before daybreak, Junior half-drunk from the night before stumbled out of Sadie's room headed to work. He strode downstairs. A few people were passed out on the tables, but for the most part, it was empty. Forgetting about the brawl, he had gotten into, he left singing and laughing about the good time he had. He didn't take notice to Buster who stood behind a tree.

Buster followed behind him, and when Junior got far enough out of sight, he grabbed him from behind and slit his throat.

It didn't take long for word to spread. Once daybreak hit the news of a young Black boy's body with his throat cut was all people were talking about. John was inside the general store when he heard two men talking about it. He knew right off that it was Junior. Without purchasing what he came for, he headed for the path where the body was found. When he arrived, the site was in chaos with both police and spectators. He inched as close as he could to determine if it was Junior. His jaw dropped, and he bolted.

He had all kinds of emotions raging at once — He was too shocked to cry. He raced into Rosie's kitchen who was prepping a whole chicken. "You all right, John?"

John stared at the floor.

"No need to hide the truth. We already know. Son listen to me. Don't you go borrowing nobody else's problems getting yourself in trouble or killed."

"It's my fault; I should have stayed there with him or made him leave with me."

"Baby listen, the day that boy was born, God knew the day he was going to die, and how he was going to die; so, you just leave it be. You hear me? Leave it be."

John didn't say anything. *I just lost my family all over again. What curse did God put on me? This is payback for my sins.*

John thought long and hard about what he should do. He decided not to contact his family. The next day, he went to the spot where Junior was murdered and sat for hours talking with Junior. "I'm sorry. I should've stayed. It's my fault you're dead. Do you want me to contact your family? I can't do that. Now, what should I do? I'm going to take care of this for you if it's the last thing I do before I die."

John took the long way home. Once there, he packed his belongings. Rosie and Jimmy came to his bedroom door.

"You don't have to leave." Rosie wiped a tear.

"I know it's time to move on. At daybreak, I'm joining the crew and going to Montgomery to work in the sawmill."

"We're going to miss you around here." Jimmy huffed. "You could wait until Ralph comes home."

"The crew moves at daybreak. I gotta go with them. Thank you both for everything."

***

John was all set to leave Phenix city, but there was one thing that he needed to do before daybreak. He waited for Jimmy and Rosie to fall asleep and slipped out the backdoor headed to ambush Buster on his way out of the gambling spot. When he did, John grabbed him from the back and touched his lips to Buster's ear. "The day you were born; God knew the day you would die."

He slit Buster's throat, picked up his belongings, and headed to the sawmill. It wasn't quite time for them to leave, so John walked to the river, took off the clothes, and washed them to remove any trace of Buster's blood. By the time he finished, it was six o'clock, so he headed to the sawmill. He arrived just in time; the trucks were getting ready to pull off. He hopped on one of the trucks and didn't look back.

13. The Girls

The trip to Montgomery took about two and a half bumpy hours in the back of the truck, but to John, it seemed like he had been riding for days because he couldn't stop thinking about the negative things that had happened to him. He committed a double homicide, not by choice but to save his own life, and because of those murders, he was probably never going to see his family again, almost kidnapped, lost his first love, and killed another man, which weighed heavy on his mind.

John promised himself that things were going to be different in Montgomery and he was going to be free from all the unwanted strains and transgressions in his life. No matter what, he would find happiness and put behind him all the horrible memories which caused him not only to be so angry on the inside but also caused him to become an alcoholic because he drank every day trying to cope.

FINDING HOME

The truck finally stopped as the rain misted. The crew arrived in Montgomery, Alabama, for a new beginning. All the Black crewmen jumped out of the back of the trucks and stretched. When John stepped off that truck, something came over him a breath of fresh air grappled him. He knew that there was something different about this place. Maybe because of the mist clean the air.

John drew in a long breath not minding the mist. *Today, my miserable life comes to an end.* He glanced at the crewman beside him. "This town is my new home. My fresh start and I'm going to make the best of it."

"Montgomery is a stopping point. Lot's more sawmills to be built." The steely eyed crewman jested as he spat tobacco.

"I don't know about that. There's something about the feel of this city. John flashed a huge smile.

The foreman pressed his fingers to his lips and blew a loud whistle. "You boys got two hours. Get you something to eat, then go to bed. We start bright and early at sunrise."

The crew busied themselves and made a make-shift camp with their things or found a place on the back of the truck to make a bed as the White men drove away to find a hotel. That didn't much matter to John. He was used to sleeping like that although he didn't have the company of Irene. He found a spot beneath a large tree, piled up some leaves to make the ground softer, and flopped down using his sack of belongings as a pillow.

As he closed his eyes, his past flashed before him. He first thought was about his cousin Junior. *Why God did you allow our paths to cross only to let him die at the hands of a jealous crook. He wasn't a bad guy, he hadn't killed anybody like me, but I'm still alive. Why? God, if you are real, will you tell his family for me? If I go back, I might get myself killed. Did you put a curse on me or am I paying for something else my momma and pappa did?*

Suddenly, he remembered the words of his pappa's firm voice. "In this life, nothing is promised. You don't always get what you give, and you don't always give what you get, but one thing for certain is this, as sure as the day you were born, you will surely die one day."

That voice inside of John's head sent chills through his body. For the first time, he became alarmed about his future. *God, do you know how I will die? Is it going to happen soon? I don't want to die. I need to make a man of myself and make my mamma proud of the man I have become.*

Somehow John's in-depth thinking session gave him a new outlook on life. He sat straight up and glanced around at the crewman who slept near. *Okay, John. For the rest of my life until the day of my last breath, I will no longer feel sorry for myself. Never again will I question God's word or his plan for me. Never again will I wonder how or why. Until the end, I will live life as it comes and just deal with it.*

The next day, John was the first to rise and went right to work. It was as if he had changed overnight because he didn't wake up thinking about his mother or feeling like something was missing in his life. He accepted his fate, his situation, and believed that God's plan would soon be revealed to him. He was finally at peace.

It only took John three days to find what he loved most, a gambling house. As always, he staked his claim, and he quickly became a regular known by the locals. Every moment he wasn't working or sleeping, he gambled, and he often broke the house. He won so much that people would not let him bring a pair of dice for nothing in the world. They swore that he was putting some spell on the game and that he must have come from New Orleans somewhere because of the swift and sometimes illegible English he spoke, but he was a simple Georgia boy with Geechee heritage -- gambling and drinking became John's life.

John neither told anybody where he lived before landing in Montgomery nor his real name. He thought it to be best that way. "Pie, that's what you can call me. That's what people back home do because I love me some peach pie. That's all you need to know about a man like me. Well, that and I'm a hard worker."

Like the other places before, John quickly set the tone for his presence. He had to let those Alabama boys know that he wasn't going to take any mess and that if they looked for trouble and came across him, they'd come out better if they passed on by him because if they stopped and picked him as a victim, then they most certainly would not come out on top. He got into a few disputes, but it only took one fight where John got double-teamed by the Brooks brothers who supposedly were the worst in the city because everybody feared them.

Once in a gambling game, the Brooks brothers accused John of cheating, and then the oldest and most obnoxious decided to snatch John's winnings out of his hand. "You don't deserve this. You're a cheater."

John quickly seized his money putting it back into his pocket and knocked the brother out cold with one punch. "No one touches my money."

When the other brother saw what had happened, he retrieved his blade from his front pocket and headed straight for John. John bolted toward him meeting him halfway, and with one solid-fisted punch, he knocked him out cold. Both brothers lay on the ground out more frigid than a block of ice.

The others watched in confusion. Some mixed with fear and wonder and others were thinking the Brooks brothers deserved it. "Way to go Pie."

"Pie, remind me never to mess around with you."

John took the blade from the one brother, nudged him with his foot to make sure he was knocked out, and then took the oldest Brook brother's shoes off his feet. "I believe these are my size." *So much for staying out of trouble and living a clean life. Sorry, God. It was a matter of life or death, and I needed those shoes.*

He pulled out his gun he stole from Jonathan Brown. He glanced around at the crewmen. "Now first thing, you'll need to do when these fools wake up is to tell them to never bring a knife to a gunfight, and if you come to fight Pie and you is more than one, it's most definitely gonna be a gunfight." He looked at everyone as he waved the gun. "I didn't cheat, and I don't ever cheat cause I don't have to."

One of the hotshot crewmen stood. "I'm out. You can take this game and shove it."

"I'm out. I don't have no more money to give you, Pie. You're just too good."

"I'm out too."

The crewmen who respected John stayed and continued to gamble. John never had to worry about anyone trying to jump him again; in fact, those Brooks brothers became good friends to John. No one knew for sure why the bond between the brothers and John but speculated that they either admired John for his courage, or they were mighty scared of his ways. Didn't matter to John; either way he was good and didn't have to worry about them anymore.

John spent almost six years working for the sawmill and had grown into a responsible and hardworking man. He somehow forgot about the sins he committed, just like he promised himself he would. Even the thoughts of his mamma, who meant the world to him, grew few and far in between. Now twenty-four, meeting the ladies was never a problem because he had what it took and they were attracted to his bad-boy ways and his looks, but after dating several, he hadn't found love. Maybe it was because he wasn't looking for it or because love just hadn't come his way with Lorretta still in the back of his mind.

He began dating Gloria, a real spit-fire beauty that most men would give everything they owned to date. There was no real love between them, and John only spent time with her on occasion. She was all right with that because she wasn't a one man's woman.

John found a shack he called home and often invited Gloria to spend the night. He gazed into her eyes as he held her close.

"You look mighty pretty tonight in that red dress."

"Why thank you, Pie. I bought it just for you."

"For me and the rest of the men you see."

"Now, Pie. Don't you be talkin' like that. You know I only have eyes for you."

"Eyes for my ways and my money."

"Honey, if you had money, you wouldn't be livin' in this shack."

"It's home, my home."

She grabbed his hand and led him to the bed. "How about a little roll in the hay?"

"I'll get us another drink."

She slipped out of her red dress and strode to the closet.

He turned around. "You know you ain't allowed to hang your clothes in my closet."

"Right, you don't want me too comfortable."

John poured two glasses of whiskey. "How about that drink?"

John forgot about his family and about all the things his mamma taught him about only dating the marrying kind of woman. He ran the women and ran the streets at night, no longer talking to God. If all the mishaps in his life had taken a toll on John, you would never know it because John seemed to be living his best life. With a little money in his pocket, something to drink, and a woman at his side, he made his place or at least that's what it seemed like from the outside. He no longer felt sad or alone because he numbed his pain through alcohol, women, and gambling.

It wasn't long before John began feeling the need for his woman, the woman that he would spend the rest of his life with, the woman that would have his children, the woman that he could take care of as a husband should. He longed for the woman who would be the apple of his eye, the woman who would cook, clean, and raise his children. One thing for certain that woman was neither Gloria nor the women he spent time within the seedy side of his life. When spending time with them, he often imagined that they were that woman, the woman that he was searching for to spend the rest of his life. Not that he wanted them to be, but he would practice how he was going to treat his woman. He knew that she would come, he didn't know how, but he knew she would come, and it wouldn't be that much longer. *It's God's plan for me.*

One night at the gambling house, in the middle of a crap game, Gloria pranced in wearing her famous red dress. She wasn't alone, or with any of the other girls she hung with, but a new girl in town. When John gazed upon her loveliness, his heart skipped a beat. For a second, he thought he was dreaming because he hadn't seen a girl like that in these parts. She was high yellow with hazel eyes, and when she opened her mouth, it seemed as if the whole room lit up because she had a mouth full of gold. John quickly forgot all about the game and the money he had in it; he strode over to Gloria and that beautiful young thang.

He paid no attention to Gloria; his heart skipped a beat as he gazed into the eyes of her friend. "What's your name?"

Before she could answer a voice from across the room, barreled John's way. "That's Fire Mouth Momma. If you ain't got the dime, she ain't got the time."

John didn't pay that comment any attention. "You get anything you want; it's on me." John hadn't been attracted to any light-skinned woman before; he always felt the blacker the berry, the sweeter the juice, and he had always pictured his wife looking just like his mother, small-framed, long hair, beautiful figure, and a God-fearing praying woman of God who would care about her family. There was something about this one; she was the most beautiful girl John had every gazed his eyes upon in his entire life.

Gloria tilted her head and winked. "How you gonna disrespect me? This is my cousin. Now, you ain't about to two time me with my blood, are you?"

John didn't even respond to Gloria; he wedged his way between Gloria and this fine thang standing near her. "You ain't got no name, or you just don't wanna tell me?"

"Ann."

"Miss Ann, you're gonna be my wife."

Ann laughed. "You don't even know me, and didn't I just hear my cousin say that you were her man?"

John turned around and glanced at Gloria, who stood behind him with her hands on her hip. She looked madder than a puffed toad frog. She was so mad that she could have knocked all his teeth down his throat and made him spit them back up one at a time. "You've got some kind of nerve, Pie."

"Pie?" Ann giggled. "What kind of name is Pie?"

John glared at Gloria. "You ain't my woman and I ain't your man."

Gloria grabbed Ann's hand. "Come on. We don't need his bad ass." She tugged Ann toward a group of gamblers, but she remained steadfast.

"You go, Gloria. I want to learn why this man is called Pie." She didn't move because John looked better to her than she did to him, and he said to her that she could have anything she wanted. That alone was like music to Ann's ears because she liked to drink, and she loved a man who had money and didn't mind sharing it with a woman.

John nodded and smiled. "Where you from, Ann, and how come I ain't never seen you before?"

"Probably because you ain't been looking for me now, what about my drink?"

"Get what your heart desires. I'd buy you the world if I could." John waved the house lady his way. "Give this pretty lady anything she wants."

"I'll take my usual."

John rubbed Ann's arm. "Miss Ann, are you hitched to somebody special?"

She pretended to be bashful as her cheeks blushed.

"If you are married, how did you get out of your husband's sight? Where do you live? Can I walk you home?"

"Do you want me to answer, or are you gonna ask questions all night?"

"It don't matter if you answer or not, as long as I can sit here in your company."

"I'm flattered. How did you come by the name Pie? That's kinda strange."

"Back where I came from, I was known to eat peach pies. That's how the name was given to me."

She batted her long black thick lashes. "I'm known to make the best peach pie ever. You like peach pies?"

"Gloria must have told you that they're my favorite."

"Not at all. Funny thing, she never mentioned you. I reckon she wanted to keep you all to herself."

"I want to taste one of those peach pies of yours."

"Pie, where are you from? How come I haven't seen you around here and where is your wife?"

"Ain't got no wife. But, you're gonna be mine, and you'll make me a peach pie every Sunday. I see it all now."

"Do you, now? That's mighty bold of you."

"A man knows when it feels right in his heart. Now tell me where you're from.

"I'm from right here in Montgomery, I'm not married, I don't have a boyfriend, and I love a man who doesn't mind taking care of his woman. Where are you from?"

"That don't matter. What matters is that I don't have a wife and you're exactly the marrying kind. My place ain't far from here. You want to go for a walk and get a private drink? Let me get to know my future wife."

"I don't know you well enough for that."

The house lady brought them their drinks.

John smiled. "After a round or two of these, you'll be changin' your mind."

They sat and talked for about two hours and drank several more rounds of whiskey.

"Pie, I'm ready. Let's go to your place."

John downed his last bit of whiskey. "Let's roll." He gently squeezed her hand and led her out the door.

It didn't take long for the two to become an item. Ann moved in with John after a month of courting, and he took care of her just like he said he would.

He worked and brought home the bacon, and she took care of the house, prepared a home-cooked meal every evening, and on Sundays, she made him a peach pie.

They sat at the small kitchen table. John took the last bite of a slice of peach pie. "Ann, you do make the best peach pie."

"Why, thank you. I try hard to keep you happy."

"One day, I'm gonna make an honest woman out of you."

"What are you waiting on?"

"It's not that I don't love you, I'm waiting on the right time. I always planned on heading north to make my life.

Not sure how you feel about that. And, now that I lost my job at the sawmill, it ain't the right time."

"My friend Blythe, the schoolteacher, says they need a janitor. You're a fine handyman."

"I'll check that out in the morning."

"Pie, I'm pregnant."

John didn't know how to react to the news and sat in silence, staring at the floor.

"Pie, we're going to have a baby."

"I better go get that job." He shoved his chair back.

"Pie, don't you want a family?"

He got on one knee. "I thought I'd be married first. I'm happy."

***

John got the job as the janitor and the job gave him enough money to support Ann. During the last week of her pregnancy, he brought food home from the school for her so she wouldn't have to cook.

Late one afternoon, John came home and discovered Ann in labor. "You okay?"

"The baby is coming. Go get help."

John ran out the door as fast as he could to a neighbor's house. Before he could return, Ann had delivered a baby girl. John kneeled beside her, kissed her, and touched the baby as his neighbor, Doris, tended to the newborn.

"She's beautiful, just like her momma." John's eyes flushed. "What are we going to name her?"

"Ethel, after my grandmother."

"It's a beautiful name."

Ethel was the apple of John's eye; there was nothing he wouldn't do for his baby girl. Every day he brought her food from the school when she got old enough to eat, and she enjoyed it. John would often tell Ann how much Ethel looked just like his mother and one of his sisters. Then she slammed the bombshell.

"Why don't we take her to see them? We've been together most two years now. The only thing I know about you is that you came from Georgia."

John never really talked much about his family. When he did, it was very brief. "I can't go back because of my sin. I killed two White men."

"I'm not surprised. You tend to have an explosive temper. Thought all this time, you must have done something really bad to stay away from your momma you love so much."

"I'm a murderer."

"Not in my eyes. You're a great man and a wonderful father. That's all I care about, especially since I'm pregnant again."

"That is some news."

"I'm worried about the money to feed another mouth."

"Don't you worry about nothing. We'll make ends meet somehow, someway."

"I've been asked by a White lady uptown to do some cooking and cleaning for her. I can bring Ethel. We can use the money."

"I don't want no woman of mine cleaning up after no White woman. You got plenty to keep yourself busy with around here."

"That won't feed a new baby."

"Then do what you want as long as it don't interfere with your jobs here."

The time came, and Ann gave birth to another girl. John insisted just as he had done with the last baby that he would pick the name. She never asked John why she just let him name them, but John had a reason for choosing the names of the babies and that was because he had called the first one after his mother and this one, after his oldest sister. Unlike most men who would want a son, John was happy with his girls because he felt that he would always be there to protect them no matter what. John loved and cherished his girls, and he would often tell Ann that if she ever left him, that his girls were staying right there with him. The girls brought John such joy; he slacked up on drinking and wasn't gambling as much either.

Through the week, he would work and then come home to be with his daughters, but the weekend was his, he would get off work on Friday evening, go home with the food he brought from the school, make sure his daughters were fed, and then he was gone. Usually until the next day or sometimes even the whole weekend.

Days, weeks, months, and years had passed, and it wasn't long before Ann and John had a house full of children; six girls. They didn't have much, but they had each other. Ann and John had gone through thick and thin and between their drinking, his gambling, and going to jail occasionally, the relationship between them ended.

John told Ann that she could leave, but his children would stay right there with him. So, she decided to wait for the sake of her girls, but after a while, she left because she feared him. He had told her all the things that he had gone through and done before he came to Montgomery and she had witnessed first-hand herself the explosiveness behind John's anger when he got mad. She had seen him get into several fights, and she knew that he would pull his blade out and use it in the blink of an eye.

John became more resentful than he was before he met Ann and they had the children. Was it because he was missing home so much or did, he feel stuck in Montgomery and his dreams of going to the city were no longer possible?

It was the worst day of Ann's life, the day she left her children with John but, she knew that if she didn't leave, John would probably kill her because of the things that she had done. Ann left when her baby girl Sarah was just two old. She left her oldest daughter Ethel to take care of the other five girls.

Although Ann was gone from the children, she always sent them gifts for their birthdays and Christmas. It wasn't much, but it was enough to let the girls know that she loved them.

John did the best he could to raise his daughters. He worked hard and made sure they had what they needed, but the stress of being a single father was undoubtedly there because John began drinking again and often came home drunk. The girls would steal money from his pockets go to the show.

When John would wake up, he would reach into his pockets to see that some of his cash was missing and he knew every time that the girls had taken it and gone to the movie theater. He walked right down to the theater and whipped their butts. Although he scolded them not to do it again, as soon as he came home drunk, they would do it again. John finally gave them each twenty-five cents to keep them from going into his pockets.

John never talked with his daughters about where he was from and why or how he ended up in Montgomery, Alabama, and they never asked. A few years passed, and nothing had changed. John was still both parents to his children, and the oldest daughter was still doing what she knew how to as far as raising the children. She made sure that they went to school and that their hair was combed every day. No social worker ever had to come to the house because the children were being taken care of, and John made sure of that. He vowed to God that he would take care of his daughters.

One night, John was at the bootlegger gambling joint, and for some reason, an uneasy feeling overcame him; something inside told him to go home, but he didn't. The gambling game was more important, and he was on a hot streak. He stayed there and continued to gamble. It seemed like that night was the best night he had since he had been betting, he was winning big. He had won big before but never like this. There was a group of men from out of town, and they were some high rollers, big money men. John could tell by the way they dressed and the type of car they drove. *I'm not leaving until every one of them are dead broke and have nothing left in their pockets but lint balls.*

He had succeeded in breaking two of the men, and they had gotten up and walked away, but there were three more, and John wanted their money too.

One of the men who had gotten up from the game came over and gave John a drink of corn liquor. John was reluctant to take it at first. "I don't take nothing from nobody I don't know."

"Well, least you can do is take a drink with the man that you just busted dry as a bone."

The man gave John the Mason jar and walked off. John took a swig of the corn liquor, sat it down, and continued gambling. He picked up the jar of corn liquor and drank every once in a while. Suddenly, the room started spinning, John started seeing double, and he started sweating profusely. Then it happened, John hit the floor aware of what was happening, but he couldn't move. He lay there with his eyes closed listening to the people as they stood over him.

One of John's friends picked him up, threw him in his truck, and drove him to the hospital. On the way, John's mind was still alert, and he tried to tell the man to make sure that his daughters were okay. Once he realized that they couldn't hear him and that he wasn't moving, John knew that it was over. He would die by being poisoned in a gambling game, and he had no way of letting anyone know what had happened to him before they left for the hospital. He saw the face of the man who had given him the corn liquor standing back laughing at him, and he couldn't do anything about it. *God, please let my children find a home one day.* He lay in the hospital for several days as his life flashed before him.

Soon, his daughters arrived at the hospital. Tears ran down John's face, and he was unable to speak.

A doctor entered the room and approached John's girls. "He won't live much longer."

"Is he in any pain?"

"No, he doesn't feel anything because he is brain dead. He may be able to hear you."

"Papa, we love you."

Eighteen years had gone by since John left home; and just as the day he was born, the day that he would die had come. Just like that John Chambless was dead.

14. Finding Home

Dead at the young age of thirty-six, John's funeral was one of confusion and horror for his kids, and with Ann, the children's mom nowhere to be found, what would be the fate of the six girls who were left behind to fend for themselves? There were no grandparents, no aunts, no uncles, or even close friends to take the girls; there was no one.

The state department of children services stepped in and decided to place the girls in group homes or an orphanage. With the girls' lives up in the air and no one caring enough to take a child until they got old enough to take care of themselves, Ethel, the oldest sister, who was only seventeen, stepped up to the plate. "My pappa would not want us apart. I'll raise my sisters myself. I'm not walking out on them like our mother did."

Ethel found a job cleaning houses for White folks and did the best she could by her sisters. She took on the responsibility of raising her sisters, and it was not easy.

Times were trying as well as confusing to all the girls; they had been dealt one hard blow after another.

The youngest daughter Sarah, and next to her, Barbara, were very close and leaned on one another during the time that they lived with their sister. After a year or so, Ann, their mother, showed up and tried to stay there with the kids.

Ethel confronted her mother. "Why did you leave us?"

"I had to. Your pappa threatened to kill me and I believed him. He had a mighty bad temper."

"You should have stayed, no matter what."

"Baby, I wanted to. I was scared. I'll make it up to all of you. You'll see."

"You still should have stayed."

"I left to save my own life. I met a man by the name of Roy and married him. I loved him very much." Ann and John had never gotten married.

"Where is he?"

"That's not important. What's important is that I'm back."

Ann was a good mother to her children. The girls were so pleased to have their mother there with them, and it was great that Ann tried to pick up where John left off raising the children, but there was just one problem. Ann had become an alcoholic, and it didn't take long before the stress of raising kids took its toll on her. She had managed to be somewhat sober while she was with the girls, but it was just too much, and she began drinking not sociably, but every day, so that put the oldest daughter right back into the position of being a mother and father to the girls.

Ann had only been there with the children in Montgomery for a few months when she sat Ethel down for a chat. "I'm leaving. I'm going back to Selma."

"You're just gonna pack up and leave us."

"I have too. I'm no good to any of you here. I should have never come back."

"You're cruel. Get out!"

"I'll come back to get them when I have a better place for them to live."

"I said get out!"

Ann left, but just as she said, she came back after four months and got the girls. She took them back to Selma with her and kept them there.

It was summer, so there was no school for the girls. They once again were happy to be with their mother, but it didn't take long for them to realize that their mother was in an abusive relationship. Roy was very rude and an alcoholic as well. Living there with Ann and Roy was almost like a routine horror story because everything would be fine during the week, but on Fridays when Roy came home, they knew what was going to happen; he'd get drunk and then beat their mother. Eventually, it got so bad that Ethel had to come and get them.

By now, Ethel had a baby, and she had a man of her own. She confronted her mother. "I'm taking my sisters back home with me where they belong."

"You can't take my babies from me."

"You watch. You're not fit and I'm not gonna stand by and let Roy ruin their lives like he has ruined yours. I'll kill him if he ever lays a hand on any of them."

"You're just like your pappa. If someone don't suit you, kill them."

"That's not fair. Pappa was a good man. Roy is not. You can come with us.

"I can't leave Roy no matter what. I love him."

"Then it's your death on his hands, not mine."

Was it really that Ann didn't want to leave her husband? Or, was it the demon of alcoholism that made her stay? Whatever the case was, Ann did not go; she stayed in Selma while Ethel took her siblings back to Montgomery.

Ethel kept her sisters for a couple of years and then rented a house for them to stay in leaving the second oldest, Evelyn Sue, in charge of the others. Times were hard for the girls but, they had each other, and that was all that mattered. They did the best they could with the little they had. As time passed, the girls got older, they began having children of their own and moving out.

Eventually, there was only Evelyn Sue, Barbara, and Sarah left there at the house. Evelyn Sue had two babies of her own by now, and she had to take care of them as well as her sisters. Then one day, she went to visit her aunt, Ann's sister, while Barbara and Sarah stayed with Ethel. Ann's sister was a bootlegger, and the scene there at her aunt's house was nothing new to Evelyn Sue because having an alcoholic for a mother and father, the girls were used to bootleggers. Evelyn Sue enjoyed the trip to her aunt's so much that she started going every weekend. On one of her visits, she met a man. His name was Charles, he came in, ordered a shot of whiskey, and told Evelyn Sue to keep the change. It wasn't long before they were an item and she had moved to Clanton with her children to live with Charles.

This meant that Barbara and Sarah had to go back and live with Ethel because they were too young to live alone. She kept them for a few years, and by now the girls had become teenagers.

They never really talked about their mother much; maybe because she was still living or perhaps because she hadn't been there for them the way that a mother should. They would often talk about their father. Maybe it was because he had taken care of them as long as he lived and gave them the love that they should have gotten from their mother. He could have easily walked away from his responsibilities of a parent as this was becoming a common thing with men, especially Black men. Not John though, even after the children's mother walked out on them, he took care of his children.

The one thing that the girls talked about most was the fact that they didn't know where their father was from or who his people were. One day Sarah wanted to know and questioned Ethel. "Do you know where Pappa came from?"

"Somewhere in Georgia."

"What part?"

"I don't know what part; all I know is Georgia."

"Was he an only child?"

"I don't know that either. He never talked about his family. He kept that to himself."

"What happens if he does? Don't you want to know? Don't you think they deserve to know how Pappa died?"

"I don't have a clue about his past. Where would we even start?"

"Before here, Pappa lived somewhere. Do you remember where?"

"Momma said he worked in a sawmill in Montgomery and she met him while he was gambling in a bootlegger joint."

"That's sounds just like Pappa."

"I miss him."

"I think we all do."

"One thing for certain, I don't miss those whippings at the movie theater."

The girls laughed.

Sarah got pregnant, and Ethel took her back to Selma to be with Ann, their mother. Sarah remained in Selma with her mother until she had her baby, then she moved to Clanton with her sister Evelyn Sue. She was still young, just fourteen, and this meant that her sister had to take on the responsibility of raising her and her new baby. She did this out of love because her husband Charles did not mind one bit, he welcomed them with open arms.

Ethel went to Selma one day and visited her mother who was in her drunken state. She packed Ann's things, didn't tell her where she was taking her, put her in the car and left.

FINDING HOME

The girls had gotten tired of the way that their mother was living and treated by her husband, so they had gotten together and came up with a plot to go and get their mother one day when they knew her husband wasn't going to be home.

Ethel took Ann to Clanton, where Evelyn Sue and Sarah were living, and she stayed there with them for a while. Leaving Selma was hard for Ann, especially because it wasn't her choice. She became very depressed and drank more than she did before she left Selma. She knew that if she went back, Roy would probably beat her to death and her daughters had told her that if she did go back, they would go after her and bring her right back, so she came to grips with being in Clanton. It wasn't long before she had her place in Clanton and began to think of it as home. Although Ann still drank, her daughters felt that she was going to be all right because she was no longer living in an abusive relationship.

Things were going about as well as could be expected, considering all that the girls had gone through, and they were women now with children of their own. One thing that each of the girls told themselves was that their children would not grow up the way that they did and that they would never leave them no matter what. In some ways, they had made Ann mom all over again because she would often have to babysit her grandchildren. There were seventeen in all, and sometimes, she would have about twelve or more at one time.

Ann's grandchildren loved her; they called her Madea. Ann adored her grandchildren as well, and she began to feel bad for the fact that she had walked out on her girls. Maybe she was trying to make up with her grandchildren for what she didn't do with her kids because she was always right there with them.

Then the day came, by the grace of God, Ann stopped drinking, and not only did she stop drinking, she got saved. She was no longer Ann the drunk, but Ms. Ann with the white tree in her yard because she had a big oak tree that she had painted as far as she could reach white. That's what people identified her with, the white tree in the yard.

Ann had always gone to church even when she was drinking. Maybe that is why she stopped drinking because no matter how she lived her life, she always gave God her time, and because of that, He must have kept His hand on her life. You see, Ann became a true woman of God, a praying, God-fearing woman. She always thanked him for something.

Evelyn Sue's children had grown up, and Sarah had three of her own. She had gotten her own little house and took care of her children. The other girls prospered too, and their talk of John had all but vanished.

Years passed, the girls raised their children, and no one ever talked about John. Then one day, Sarah's daughter, Jessica, who was her second child became inquisitive. "Momma, who's your father?"

"His name was John Chambless. He raised me and your aunts until the day he died."

"How did he die?"

"I'm not really sure. I heard that he was poisoned by a man who lost a whole lot of money to him. I was seven at the time, and everyone kept quiet about it."

"Where was he from?"

"Somewhere in Georgia. Don't really know much. Don't even know if he had kin, but us girls."

"So, you don't know any of your family?"

"I know my mother's family, but not my father's."

"Well, don't worry, when I grow up, I will find your family for you." She was just ten years old at the time.

When she turned nineteen, Jessica along with her sister Greta had gone to live with their grandmother Ann because Sarah was married to a soldier and the girls had gotten too old to travel with them. Although Ann had only a one-bedroom apartment, it was just enough room for the three of them.

Greta, Jessica's younger sister, worked at a restaurant and Jessica joined the National Guard. Ann would wake the girls up early every morning by praying and talking to God. Her prayers would be so loud and long that the girls would lay still and listen. Sometimes they laughed at what Ann prayed for, especially when she prayed for the people who were on crack cocaine.

One day, Jessica sat on the front porch talking to her grandmother Ann, as she often did. "Madea, how did you meet my grandfather?"

"At a bootlegger gambling joint. It was love at first sight for him. He said he knew I would be his wife."

"Did you love him?"

"Of course, I loved him."

"Did you ever meet his kinfolk?"

"I know he had some, but never met them. I asked him often to take me to meet them, but he never did. Only thing he said, he couldn't go back because he had killed a White man."

"No way."

"I don't know if there's any truth in that story, but I do know he never would go back."

"Do you think he killed that White man?"

"John was a good man and a great father. if it wasn't for him, I don't know what would have happened to my children."

"I'm going to find his people. I need to know where I came from. I'm going to start by looking up every John Chambless I can find."

"I'm not even sure if that was his real name, so I wouldn't even know how to tell you where to begin looking for your grandfather's family."

"I'll find his family."

"Well look who is here."

"I'm glad Ethel came to visit. Maybe she'll know."

Jessica waited patiently for Ethel to get out of the car before she bombarded her with questions. "Do you know who John Chambless is?"

"Of course, I do, he's my pappa."

"Where is he from? Do you know his family? Why did he come to Alabama?"

"Whoa, enough with the questions. I just got here. A simple hello would be nice."

"Hello. Now did John Chambless have a family or not? If he does, I'm going to find them."

"You do that for me, and you will make me the happiest woman in the world. I've always wished to know my pappa's people."

Those words never left Jessica, and every time she saw Ethel, they talked about her finding John's family. Years passed, and Jessica eventually moved to Phenix City, Alabama, then to Columbus, Georgia. She often saw people who resembled her mother or one of her aunts, and she wondered if they were related to a John Chambless, or if they weren't connected, had they ever heard of him.

Many years had passed since John had died, and the sisters themselves were up in age. Ethel, lived in a nursing home, and when Jessica visited her, she would always ask if she had found out anything about her daddy's people. "I want you to do that for me before I die."

"I haven't forgotten. I'm still looking." Jessica, who had become a true woman of God, often prayed and asked God to lead her to her grandfather's family before her mother or one of her aunts passed. Using a copy of an old census report with John's parents, his brothers, and sisters and John listed on it, she tried to locate any of his family. She looked them up using the phone book all without luck. Then, she took a trip to Monroe Georgia and visited the archives room looking for either of their names. She looked for arrest records and anything else she could find; all futile.

The more Jessica looked, the more interested she became in finding out who John Chambless was and where he was from. She spent countless hours and exhausted all avenues trying to find her grandfather's family, but it seemed the more she searched, the further she was away from finding them.

It had been precisely one hundred years to the date that John Chambless had left home when Jessica, one day, went on a family history resource site as she had done several times in the past. She typed in her grandfather's name and low and behold, something popped up. The Chambless family had a family reunion, and the branch with John's name on it said unknown. At first, she searched all over the page to make sure that these were the right people, but deep down on the inside, she knew that it was. She prayed and asked God to show her a sign if it really was her grandfather's family and as soon as she finished, she looked at the computer and there it was, the same census report she had for years.

Jessica called her mother with the news; she told her that she had found some of her grandfather's people. She then called Ethel and told her. Even though Jessica hadn't confirmed or spoken with any of the people that she saw on the site, her heart was filled with joy mainly because with the help of God, she had done what she promised her aunt she would do, and that was to find some of her daddy's people before she died.

When Jessica told Ethel the news, all she could do was cry. The story rolled like a wheelbarrow through the family that Jessica had found some of John's people. One morning, Jessica woke up, and the first thing that came to her mind was that she needed to contact the people that she had seen online, so she started sending out emails -- "Hello, my name is Jessica Sims. I am looking for my grandfather's family. His name was John Chambless; he was born in 1902. He left Georgia many years ago, and no one knows why. I have a copy of the census report that was listed on your page, and it is an exact match to the one I have. If this sounds familiar to you, if you have a long lost relative by the name of John Chambless, please contact me at the phone number and email address provided."

Jessica was so anxious to hear from some people she had messaged that she checked her inbox two or three times a day. After a few days, she sort of lost interest because she hadn't heard from anyone.

About two weeks later, she went onto the site and there it was; a message from a woman that told her she was married to John's great-nephew. She contacted a family member. The message informed her that the woman didn't know anything about the situation because she lived in another state and that she had come to Georgia for a family reunion that the Chambless' had a couple of years back and that was when they did the family tree. Then, she listed the names of several other relatives and provided their emails.

Jessica quickly wrote back and thanked the lady. She spent the next several hours composing emails to family members the lady told her about. After sending the emails, she received a response almost immediately. She told the lady the story of her grandfather and how he had left Georgia. The girl who was around Jessica's age had heard the story of John, so she gave Jessica another number to call. She ended up speaking with one of John's great-nieces. They talked on the phone for what seemed like forever, and even though they had just met, it seemed like they had known each other all their lives. They both had so many questions that neither of them had the answer to because John had left before she was born and his parents along with all his siblings were dead.

The phone calls started pouring in, and the more Jessica talked with her new family members, the more John Chambless became a part of history to her. One of John's nieces told Jessica that her grandmother talked about John all the time and that she thought that the Klu Klux Klan had killed him. So, she died thinking her young son had been killed by the Ku Klux Klan when he had run away to another state not far from her at all because he had killed the very ones that she thought had killed him. She never knew that he had lived for several years after he had gone missing and had started not a family but an entire generation. She never got to know that the one thing she always warned her sons against, gambling, yet they loved so much, was the very thing that had taken, not one, but two of her son's lives.

Jessica told the lady that John had started an entire generation with six daughters, their children, and so on. It wasn't long before she called her aunt with the good news that she had found her daddy's people. Ethel was so shocked that she couldn't say anything, she just held the phone and wept because deep down inside, she didn't think that it was going to happen. She didn't believe that she would get a chance to see her daddy's family before she died. It wasn't long after that; the family planned a trip to go and visit their newfound family. It was a gathering to meet the John Chambless children, and although he was not there to see that home for the Chambless family had been found. At the reunion, Jessica visualized her family members who had gone on to Heaven sitting at a ballgame, watching the last ending and their team was in the lead with a sure win.

"Find your purpose in the true adventure of faith."

ABOUT THE AUTHOR

Jessica Sims is a poet, writer, and author of the novel *Finding Home*. A professionally trained (88M) US Army and Corrections Officer Georgia Department of Corrections, studied accounting at George C Wallace, Social and Criminal Justice and is a Minister of the gospel of Jesus Christ. She has spent the last few years reading and writing novels that bring her characters to life leaving readers imaginations with a twist of uncertainty to sheer certainty. She started out writing songs and quickly realized that she had a real love for the art of storytelling. Jessica lives in Phenix City, Alabama, where she is enjoying the retired life and spending time with her grandchildren, Amere and Jessica.

Her drive is to write books that readers will want to read from beginning to end without putting down. With her extended stays in several states and living in the Republic of Panama growing up as a military brat, Jessica is versatile and can relate to all people on all levels. Being born in Alabama in a small town during a time when segregation was still accepted, Jessica was able to put her heart into her debut novel *Finding Home*.

"Find your purpose in the true adventure of faith."

Jessica Sims Email: jssjrs@yahoo.com.

FINDING HOME

Be sure to subscribe to Jessica's blog at:

https://www.jessicasims.blogspot.com/